CONTROL MEASURES

If you've lost control,
it's time to get it back.

ISBN-13: 978-1-890305-43-7
ISBN-10: 189030543X

Copyright 2017 by Seth A. Hulse. All rights reserved.
First Edition, Paperback
Published October, 2017
Published by Gold Rush Publishing
PO Box 582155, Elk Grove, CA 95758
http://goldrushpub.com

Seth Hulse, CLC
Founder, Control Measures Life Coaching
Certified Life Coach, Leadership Coach,
Motivational Speaker, Author
www.controlmeasureslifecoaching.com

Disclaimer: The opinions expressed in this book are solely those of the author.

Contents

Preface 11

Forword 15

Dedication 17

Thank You 19

Testimonials 21

Introduction 23

    Me (Myself and I) 23

Chapter 1: Self-Esteem Maximum Booster 39

    Section 1: I like me and I agree. (Check Mate, Game Over, I Win, Case Closed) 39

    Section 2: Body Image (One size does not fit all.) 42

    Section 3: The Real Us (Who are you now? Who do you want to be? What are the differences?) 45

    Section 4: Days, Weeks and Months (A great time for change.) 47

    Section 5: Stand Your Ground - (Believe me, your beliefs are worth believing. Believe it.) 51

    Section 6: Self-Improvement Made "Easy" (A little at a time and nothing is off limits) 54

    Section 7: Rocky Balboa's Hard-Hitting Wisdom (Sandra' story) 60

    Section 8: Rambo's Motivation (What's your something?) 70

    Section 9: A way to like exercise (It sounds crazy I know) 73

Chapter 2: Parenting 101 75

    Section 1: Young Children (Basic Training) 75

Section 2: Respect (No one dies from saying Sir, Ma'am, please and thank you.) 77

Section 3: Parenting (A verb - A contact sport never requiring a computer.) 81

Section 4: Intervention (Sweat the Small Stuff) 83

Section 5: If/Then (The Accountability Guarantee) 85

Section 6: Bad, Good and Exceptional (Correct, Recognize and Reward) 87

Section 7: Obi Wan Kenobi (Why parents and their kids don't see things eye to eye) 89

Chapter 3: Teen Truths 91

Section 1: Responsibility (Stupidly Stuff is Important) 91

Section 2: The 14th Year (Childhood Is Over! It's about time. Aren't you glad?) 96

Section 3: Turning from Childhood (Accepting Reality – Proving Yourself Worthy) 97

Section 4: Disrespect (Keep it to yourself) 97

Section 5: The Big Lie (Adolescence) 98

Section 6: "Boys will be Boys" (Lawsuits will be Lawsuits) ... 99

Section 7: The 18-Year-Old (It's only a number.) 100

Section 8: True Friends (Your Best Interest Investment) 101

Section 9: Your Comfort Zone and the Dog Leash (Who really has control and why?) 102

Section 10: Your Friends the Guinea Pigs (They'll show you what not to do.) 106

Section 11: Verbal Bullies (Predictable - How do they know all this stuff? – It's all about me!) 106

Section 12: Cyber Bullies (More chicken than verbal bullies.) 111

Section 13: Physical Bullies (The line has been crossed.) 111

Section 14: The Mechanic and the Dentist (Check your advice givers number.) 115

Section 15: The High Bar (Have quality in your life) 117

Section 16: The Age Difference (We're all the same at the same time.) 118

Section 17: Privacy (The best way to protect your privacy.) . 118

Section 18: Privacy, The Sequel (Someone is looking for you.) 120

Section 19: Reactions (Yours determines theirs.) 122

Section 20: It Takes Time (You'll be here anyway) 124

Section 21: Been There, Didn't Do That (Surviving the lie) . 125

Section 22: My Life is Crap – Send (Well, hmmm, not everyone has a cell phone) 126

Section 23: D-O for the B-O (Do you smell something?)...... 127

Section 24: Words from the Toilet (I am not kidding) 128

Section 25: Being taken seriously (Walk their walk and talk their talk) 131

Section 26: Invisible Good Advice (The forest and the trees) 134

Section 27: How to solve pretty much any problem (Time Travel) 137

Section 28: Hating what you're doing (It's Ok) 138

Chapter 4: Relationships 141

Section 1: The Good, the Bad and the Ugly (Let's take a ride) 141

Section 2: Jerkectomy (Boy Friends/Girl Friends Part I) 144

Section 3: The Alphabet Test (Boy Friends/Girl Friends Part II) 144

Section 4: Justification (They'll prove you right.) 145

Section 5: How much more can you take? (It's a matter of time) 146

Section 6: Bad People and Your Life (DO NOT let them in.) 148

Section 7: Our Story (Time – Connections – Love) 150

Section 8: Surface Decisions (Emotions) 164

Section 9: Taking Turns (Don't) 166

Section 10: No Company (Better than Bad Company) 167

Section 11: Broken (Together) 169

Chapter 5: Listen Up, Men 170

Section 1: Her (Single Minded Obsession – Absolute Devotion – Pride – Protection – Love) 170

Section 2: Where have the gentlemen gone? (Man Skills 101 – Don't forget to teach the boys.) 171

Section 3: Superheroes (Like Us) 176

Section 4: Sheep, Wolves and Sheep Dogs (Hint: You should be the Sheep Dog, not the Wolf) 177

Section 5: Macho Man (I hope you're not) 178

Section 6: The Pedestal (Hi Babe!) 179

Section 7: Because it's Wednesday (or whenever) 183

Section 8: Male vs Men (Polar Opposites) 185

Chapter 6: The Home 189

Section 1: Ownership (It belongs to you, not your kids.) 189

Section 2: The Lord giveth and the Lord taketh away. (So can you) 192

Section 3: The Disappearing Act (How to keep your house clean.) 194

Section 4: Being a part or being apart. (Family Survival) 194

Section 5: The Minimum Law (Everything else is conditional) 198

Section 6: Spock (Vulcan Family Priorities) 200

Chapter 7: Miscellaneous, Random, Generic, Non-Specific Stuff.. 203

    Section 1: The Fault Game (Lay fault where it truly belongs and call it what it is!) 203

    Section 2: They're asking for it. (The Adult Translation)...... 206

    Section 3: Your Thank Account (How much do you owe?) .. 212

    Section 4: $1,000 (Is it really necessary?).............................. 219

    Section 5: 80 Per centers (Hey, pick up my slack!) 220

    Section 6: Bosses (Are they good enough for you?).............. 221

    Section 7: Color (It's only skin deep) 225

    Section 8: Heroes (They're not who you think.) 226

    Section 9: Wants and Needs (Not in that order.).................... 230

    Section 10: Money (Where does it all go?) 231

    Section 11: Discrimination (Don't do it but profile like crazy!) 231

    Section 12: Taking Time Off (AKA: Quitting)...................... 234

    Section 13: Good Things (Looking Forward) 235

    Time to go (Wrapping it up.) 236

Connect with Seth 237

Preface

Well, here we go – my first book. I have to tell you, the style of this book isn't in line with the normal way others do this book writing thing. I'm not worried about it. I care about helping people more than sailing a pre-navigated course on my maiden voyage through the literary world. Actually, this is our voyage isn't it, so let's go. I hope you'll enjoy the uniqueness of what lies ahead.

What lies ahead is a collection of topics I've spoken about to individuals, couples, families and groups since 1988. You may experience a different feel depending on the topic you're reading. That's because they're written in the same way they've been spoken. It will be like you're reading the transcript from a speech or monologue.

Some have a definite "in your face" tone. That's because when the words were spoken I was in someone's face or the faces of a group who were the focus of the topic. Please don't be offended by this. I call people names sometimes. Please don't throw the book away. There are times when calling someone a name or leveling an insult is actually productive. These are very specific instances, though. Live and in person, they make sense. Reading them however, require understanding and the ability to put you as the reader within the environment in which the message was being given.

For the vast majority of those times the name, insult or caricature used is done so as a "serious joke." They're meant to lighten the mood but maintain the seriousness of the topic. For instance, I've called guys Neanderthals for not helping around the house or expecting their wives to wait on them hand and foot when their wives have hands and feet that need to be waited on. That's a "cave man" mentality to me, therefore, they are like cave men, therefore, I call them a cave man name, Neanderthals.

By the way, the guys I've declared to be Neanderthals usually laughed when they heard it. Actually, they laughed and grunted for their own comic effect but got the point I was trying to make. No harm, no foul.

There are times when I talk directly at, not to, a person or specific group. Again, this is done on purpose. I'm a pretty direct guy and feel there are times when straight forward directness is the only way to get the point across with the intensity it deserves. As I said, this book is like the transcript from a monologue with very specific examples used at different times.

I use a lot of disclaimers. It's kind of like a running gag throughout the book. I use so many because I find them to be funny and because people are so sensitive these days. The terms, names and descriptions used not so long ago are considered taboo and scary by many people both young and old today. Wait; can I use the terms "young" and "old" without opening up a can of sensibility? We'll see. For the same reasons, I use quotation marks quite often. This is done to make sure what lies within those marks isn't taken at absolute, literal, concrete and legally binding face value.

I've been known to use slang and make up my own words on occasion. I do this when no actual word will quite do and because they sound a little weird. For example, I use the prefix "un" before words which traditionally don't have it. That prefix indicates the opposite of the word's meaning, such as, unwrap means the opposite of wrap. Of course, my usage of "un" usually carries with it a distinct smart-alecky tone as in telling a guy who forgets his girlfriend or wife's birthday to un-dork himself. I know it's not Standard American English but I'm actually part Austrian and British with a bit of Cherokee mixed in so I'm not standard either. All joking aside, my made-up words are part of who I am and my approach when speaking to others so they're part of this book as well.

Some of the topics ahead are motivating and others may make you smile, laugh or even cry. My style of speaking is often determined by who I am to the listeners, the listeners themselves and the topics. My writing is the same way.

For example: When I was in the Air Force, I worked in Correctional Custody for a time. I was an authoritarian to the airmen sentenced there. The topics re-established military authority over them and the information was given at a loud volume, one millimeter from their faces, without question or debate.

On the other hand, I've been a life coach to those suffocating from bad relationships. Of course, I wasn't an authoritarian to them but a compassionate listener. The topics were initiated by them and the conversations were calm and reassuring.

Since this book speaks directly to different types of people, the teen topics read as if I'm talking to a teenager, not their parents. Likewise, topics for men are written as if the guys are sitting in front of me. So don't be confused if you feel I'm talking to someone else, I may be, but please read on. It may be helpful to someone you know.

Simply put, this book is my take on problems and their possible solutions, questions and their possible answers, confusion and possible clarification and more. Notice, I said "possible." My way is not the only way, neither is anyone else's. You must decide the right way for you. There are times we can't decide what to do next. We don't have a clue what our way is anymore. We need a new outlook. I use a puzzle analogy a lot to explain this.

Our lives are like puzzles and we spend our emotions and energy trying to make every piece fit. There are times though when we just stop. We reach a point we can't find a spot for a single piece anymore. We look and look, sometimes trying to force a piece where it doesn't belong (usually damaging it in the process) then, we want to give up. We can sit for hours staring at the puzzle convinced the pieces left over belong to a different puzzle, then, here comes someone else. They walk up to us, take a look at our puzzle, pick up a piece (sitting right under our noses) and say, "this might go here" and lay it in place. They walk off and we throw our chair at them. Not really.

They see our puzzle through new eyes, eyes that aren't tired and blurry from staring at it for so long. Their minds aren't confused from the many shapes and sizes before them and their emotions aren't frayed from having dealt with the puzzle for, oh say, all their life like we have. They see a piece out of place and a place it might fit. That's what this book might do for you; give you a new way to look at your puzzle.

Forword

Move in this direction by simply turning the page. Yes, you're right, that's actually a metaphor for re-gaining control. I also mean it literally. Go ahead…

Dedication

To the person who's losing or has lost control; you are extremely important and deserve to be happy, as you define it, in all areas of your life. I dedicate this book to you.

Thank You

To my Lord and Savior Jesus Christ

To my wonderful wife Cathy who is my best friend and my happiness. You have been God's greatest gift to me here on earth. I cherish and adore you.

To Jennifer Ertel for her editing prowess and advise.

To my good friend Mark Arsenault who published this book for me. I encourage everyone to check out, as I do, what Mark has to say at MarkTruth.com. Mark also heads up a great non-profit at Success-Reentry.com.

Testimonials

When my family and I first met Seth, our lives were not our own. They were controlled and filled with the aftereffects of years of emotional pain and the constant turmoil dealt out by an angry misguided teenager. Through Seth's guidance, we were able to take back control of our daily lives and start our healing process. The gentle and informative way he taught us was exactly what we needed. His support throughout this process has been a Godsend!

– S. Branham

Seth taught me what confidence is and how to believe in myself. When I first met him I couldn't look a single person in the eye because I had no self-worth and didn't feel I could do anything right. With his constant praise he taught me I was worth more than I could possibly imagine. He gave me confidence to make it through my senior year of high school. I now instill what I learned from him to my own children. Thanks to Seth, no matter what I face in life I hold my head high.

– N. Herr

I was one of Seth's original Color Guard members and he was like a father figure to me. He praised me when I did right, scolded me when I did wrong and redirected me when I was lost. I spent countless hours talking to him about some of my life issues and learned many things from him. He taught me responsibility and how to work through fear; on the other side of fear is a reward. He shaped me into the man I am today, a Lieutenant Firefighter, Training Officer and EMT.

– B. Williams

Seth's coaching provided my son growth and achievement giving him purpose and direction. I know my son is a better man today as a result of the life changing experiences Seth provided him.

– K. Schumacker

I now realize that because of Seth's guidance, the last three years of high school changed my son's life for the better. For that I owe him a huge thank you. I always loved the life lessons Seth shared with my son and his friends. I believe the biggest lesson my son learned was responsibility. Seth would always say "If you see something that needs to be done, just do it, don't wait to be asked." Seth raised my son's self-esteem. From the bottom of my heart, I thank him.

– D. Plumer

One thing that has always stuck with me has been Seth's lesson of never giving up on yourself or your dreams. I feel extremely blessed and honored to have met such an amazing man and his wonderful wife. They both have truly changed my life.

– I. Anderson

Introduction

Me (Myself and I)

Hi. My name is Seth Hulse and I'd like to thank you for reading my book. It's called Control Measures because control is something we all want and need but don't always have. When things get out of control it's bad, really bad. In personal and family relationships, control of this or that can lead to problems or the dissolution of the relationship. Controlling people are difficult to be around. Control of finances can cause manipulation of others. Control of emotions (or lack of it) can take people to great highs or great lows. Control is that important.

No one but you should have control over the many aspects of your life. You may allow another person to guide you, even to the point of making the lion's share of the decisions. The fact they do this must be because you want them to. You, of course, can take that ability away from them at any time. That's control. If you've lost control of part of your life, this book might help.

So, who am I and what business do I have writing a book anyway? Here's my pedigree. First, I am a Christian. Second, I am a husband to Cathy and the most blessed man alive. Third, I am a father of two, Sandra and Luke and a grandfather of four, Laiken, Caydense, Landon and Aiden. I'm also a United States Air Force veteran.

I grew up in central Indiana, an itsy bitsy town called Selma. My family consisted of my parents, Sam and Sue, my brother Sam Jr. with a couple dogs and many cats joining us over the years. I had a good childhood. I made some friends and was

The Hulse clan 2016; my dad Sam, mom Sue, brother Sam Jr. and yours truly.

active at school and in my church youth group. I graduated from Wapahani High School in 1983; Go Raiders!

After graduation I spent the next year trying to be gainfully employed. The economy was bad and so were the prospects of such employment, so off to the recruiters I went. I joined the US Air Force in 1984 as a Law Enforcement Specialist in the Security Police career field and was stationed at Sheppard Air Force Base in Texas.

After graduating from basic training and the Air Force Law Enforcement Academy, I was sent for ground combat training. Yes, people in the Air Force actually fight - on the ground - with guns and everything. Hey, somebody has to protect the jets and the bombs and the nuclear weapons. It was winter and it was frigid but I graduated, frostbite, trench foot and all.

I went back to my base and a couple years later I was sent to the Middle East. I protected secret things on a remote base in the middle of nowhere. I snorkeled in the Red Sea, sailed down

Here I am sporting the 80s vintage "chocolate chip" style battle dress uniform in my underground hooch called "Hill Street." I spent six months at Wadi Qena on an old Russian (Soviet Union era) air base reclaimed by the USAF. The site was called Coronet Mallard then changed to Coronet Teal. It was in the middle of nowhere Egypt and could only be resupplied by air. Yes, the Australian style turned up brim was a Wadi trademark.

I met Mohamed Ali in 1986 on a tour I took. He gave me a number representing his name and told me he'd always remember which number I was. The next time you're in Luxor visiting King Tut, ask him which number I am; he should say I'm number 30.

Say hello to my four-legged desert taxi, "Michael Jackson."

the Nile, ran up and down the pyramids, bought a lot of souvenirs and made many friends. The whole Nile and pyramids thing probably gave away what country I was in but let's just keep that to ourselves shall we? After all, it's a "secret."

When I returned to the good ol' USA I attended the Non-Commissioned Officer's Preparatory Course and graduated as Honor Graduate. What synched the Honor Graduate spot for me, according to an instructor, was my professional bearing (demeanor) and willingness to speak up and argue my side of a topic with the other students. When I say argue, I mean, quote a regulation and explain the bigger picture. I'd also explain the fundamental reasons why things had to be done a certain way and the negative outcome if they weren't. I was a cop after all, it came naturally.

Shortly after graduating from that course, I was promoted to sergeant and assigned as a cadre (fancy word for supervisor) at our base Correctional Custody Facility. It was where airmen were sent for breaking big rules or not conducting themselves to Air Force standards. It was a blend of basic training all over again, and jail. I was the second shift cadre leader. The second shift by design was a nightmare for the airmen. I was the monster within the nightmare. It was my job, so I did it.

As time moved on I went to combat exercises (war games) in Oklahoma, Arkansas and California, attended classes of all kinds, shot weapons of all kinds, became a weapons armorer and performed police duties of all kinds.

Doing cop stuff means dealing with people at their worse while conduction yourself at your best. The people who call the cops (or have the cops called on them) are often, drunk, belligerent, argumentative, crying, hurt, combative, confused and so on, but they all need help. They need to be calmed down so they can talk coherently about what has just happened. The real cause of the problem may not be what it seems when you first get out of your patrol car, it takes a little digging. It's the same way in our lives. We often feel a flood of emotions because we've been wronged and want justice. Maybe our lives are unfulfilled and we can't figure out why. We need to calm down, look at the hard facts and dig deep. Sometimes, that's the only way to determine the real cause(s) of our problems and regain control over a situation that's gotten way out of hand.

Heading out to patrol the streets of Shepherd Air Force Base, Texas.

My last major assignment was as Non-Commissioned Officer in Charge of Entry and Exit Control. Basically, I selected, trained and supervised the cops who controlled entry to and exit from the base. It was called SPOL-E or Security Police Office of Law Enforcement – Echo Flight. Some called it the

"Elite Gate Section" because it was manned by "Elite Gate Guards." Others just called it the "Egg Flight" for short. We didn't like those names very much. We just called ourselves the gate section and I was considered its unofficial Flight Chief.

For me, it was finally a day shift assignment where I only had to work 14 to 16 hours per day - answer to seemingly everyone on base with any gripe or complaint about anything they could possibly think of - even if it had nothing whatsoever to do with coming on or leaving Sheppard Air Force Base. I also went from never having supervised anyone to supervising 14 airmen. This was, of course, before I was even sent to supervisor's school to learn how to be an effective and professional supervisor. That's when I realized the Air Force had a strange sense of humor.

Actually, it all went pretty well. I had good airmen working for me (my publisher included) and good support from my immediate supervisor. Within three months we were the highest rated unit of its kind amongst Air Training Command bases. Three months later SPOL-E was given to a newly promoted Master Sergeant. Three months after he took over, it was disbanded. The Air Force's sense of humor at work again, I guess.

After leaving the Air Force, I worked in private and corporate security. I was an assistant to a Private Investigator, did a little VIP protection work (body guard) and began motivational speaking to teens.

Sergeant Hulse in 1990. Was I ever really that young?

I've written, directed and acted in numerous church plays and holiday productions. I even created a clown character named Henry Hobo. He's a good guy, a little down on his luck like all hobos but he's happy just making people laugh. I graduated from clown school and have performed as a professional clown when my schedule allows.

Me portraying Jesus during one of the Easter plays I've written.

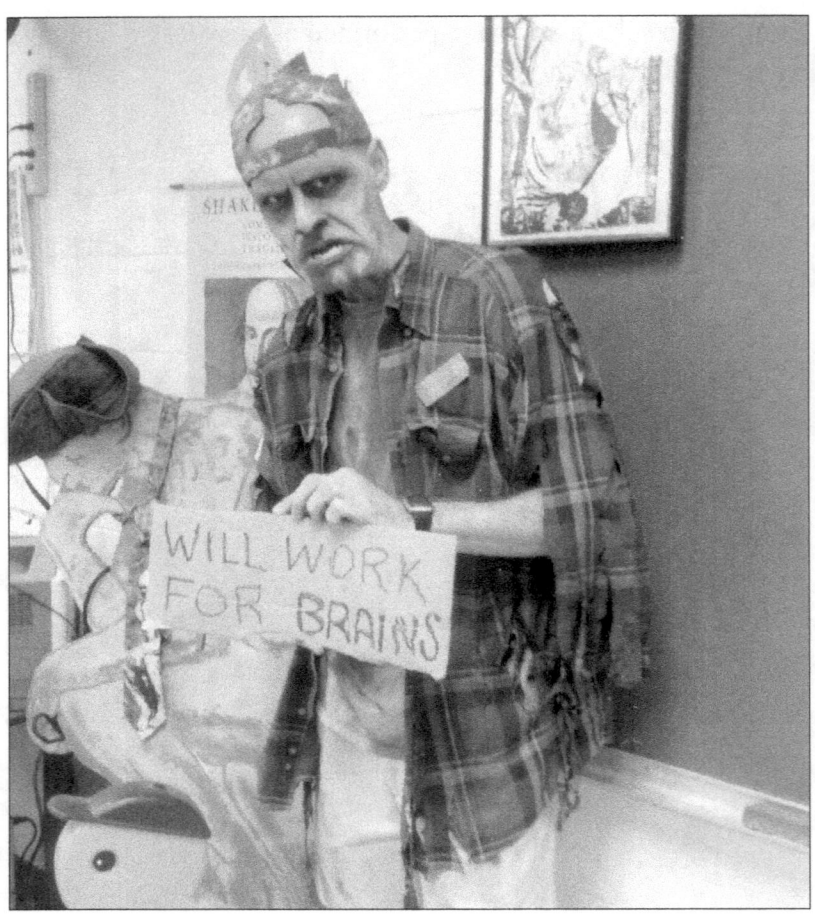

Here I am having some fun at school during homecoming week. It was zombie day of course. I noticed the kids in my classes were much better behaved that day.

I'm also a Darth Vader impersonator. BTW: Vader isn't ticked off all the time because of the dark side of the force; it's because the stupid helmet is so hot! You'd force choke everyone around you too once the temperature of your head reached critical mass. However, a couple German manufactured helmet cooling fans can make Mr. Vader a happy camper – sort of.

I didn't grow up with guns but the Air Force introduced me to them and insisted I carry one on duty. I was a natural shot. I shot expert each time I went to the range while in the Air Force no matter what the weapon was and became an armorer once I was promoted to Sergeant. I shot a perfect score on an Ohio Peace Officer Training Counsel automatic pistol course I had to take for a private security job after the Air Force. I also became Range Master for one of the security companies I worked for.

I was the study hall supervisor for Jennings County High School in North Vernon, Indiana for 18 years. I had pretty large classes. They were filled with other people's teenagers between the ages of 14 and 18. I also spent time as the school's Attendance and Truancy Officer.

In 2003 I founded, coached and was Senior Drill Instructor for the school's independent, quasi-military Color Guard. My wife Cathy coached as well. We carried the National Colors and other flags before the public for the National Anthem. We also marched in parades, performed special ceremonies like laying a wreath at the Tomb of the Unknown Soldiers in Arlington National Cemetery and traveled to places like professional sports arenas to do our duty. We were invited to perform for both games of the Indiana Boys' State Basketball Championships four consecutive years which no school color guard had done in the history of Hoosier high school basketball. We performed on the steps of the Lincoln Memorial, as well as, for celebrities like the Harlem Globetrotters and the U.S. Marine Corps Silent Drill Team.

The Color Guard met Indiana Governor (now Vice President) Mike Pence before the start of the 2016 Rolling Thunder Motorcycle Ride from the Indianapolis War Memorial to Washington DC. We had performed for the opening ceremony.

Here we are lined up for inspection prior to marching in the 2016 VJ Day Parade in Seymour, Indiana.

Each year before a game I explain to new Color Guard members that each of us is stitched into the flag. The flag represents our entire nation (the good and the bad) and each of us as individuals. This talk took place in September of 2017.

Respect

The Color Guard after a performance in our three different uniforms; dress blues, service shirt and pants and camouflage, aka, BDU, sometimes called battle dress uniform. This was after a home football game. The folded flag is to honor all who have died in the defense of this nation.

Cathy and I teach a Mixed Martial Arts Self-Defense program I founded in 2010. We teach groups and individual clients. The program covers personal self-defense (hand to hand), residential defense (locks, lights, alarms, deterrents, safe rooms, etc.) and self-defense with handguns (legal considerations, safety, concealed carry, shooting techniques, after shooting actions, etc.). It's a "menu program," by that I mean an individual person or group can choose what area or areas they want to learn depending on their needs.

In September of 2017, I became a Local Board Member for Indiana (Region 1) of the Selective Service System (Draft Board). If the US enacts a military draft again, I'll help decide if a selectee receives a waiver or not. My application had to be approved by the Governor of Indiana, then it was sent to Washington. The certificate I received (and every other board member I assume) was signed by the Director of Selective Service on behalf of The President. Pretty cool.

I'm a certified life coach and founder of Control Measures Life Coaching. I'm also a leadership coach, motivational speaker and author of this book with more to come.

So, there you have it, or me to be more precise. I've told you all this to be open and honest. You didn't know me when you picked up this book. I hope you feel you do now. A great deal of my life has been spent helping others. I wanted to help them then and I want to help you now.

Right now may be the perfect time for you to face your difficulties and problems and take back control. I hope this book helps you do just that. Let's get started.

Chapter 1: Self-Esteem Maximum Booster

Section 1: I like me and I agree. (Check Mate, Game Over, I Win, Case Closed)

I am awesome! How do I know this? I just said it. Not only did I say it, I meant it. So what brings me to this conclusion you might ask? After all, others might disagree. First, I don't need others to agree with me (except my wife and she thinks I'm awesome). Second, I know me better than anyone else (except my wife and she thinks I'm awesome). So, if I (the expert on me) think I'm awesome, then the expert (which is me) has spoken and the only logical conclusion is, I am awesome. Ta Da!

Many people have been told to their faces or by the actions of others they aren't worth much, won't amount to much, have no future, are stupid, ugly, unwanted and a truck load of other hurtful, hateful and wrong garbage. It happens so many times they think it's true. That's called a cognitive distortion, by the way. Often these things are said from the insecurities, jealously and just plain ignorance of the garbage talkers. Maybe the garbage-talkers don't want the other person to advance themself because they'd become more than the garbage-talker is. They might attract new friends which could make their current friends feel yucky, if their current friends are the garbage talkers. Odd thing; their new friends could become friends with their old friends if given a chance. Fat chance of that if their current buddies are too immature. Whatever it is, it's a bad reason for an insult. In fact, there are no good reasons for an insult. Did you get that? There are no good reasons to insult you.

Let's figure this out. If what the garbage talkers say comes from insecurities, jealousy and/or ignorance, then it can't be accurate. Therefore, it isn't true. Therefore (again) the opposite must be true. Therefore (last time) you are awesome!

You know you have talents, hopes and dreams. The garbage talkers have the talent to talk garbage and a hope you'll believe them and the dream you'll stay down where they want you. You should like you for the talents, hopes and dreams that perhaps only you know you have. Listen to yourself about you. Others will talk, let them. It's not like you can really stop them. Don't listen to them or spend an ounce of energy because of what they say. Instead, remind yourself of what the expert on you says, and that is, you are awesome!

The alphabet is filled with a bunch of letters. That's why it's called the alphabet I suppose. A couple of them are actually words all by themselves like "A" and "I." People use words (which are crammed full of these letters) to hurt us. It's not the letter's fault; it's the people's fault.

Well, I've done something awesome, which should come as no surprise. I've re-written the alphabet as it relates to me. This has given each letter a way to express itself properly. It can relate exactly the same way to you if you'll let it. It might even make your self-esteem meter head straight to overload.

Finally, the letters of our alphabet have been fortified with awesome. Please notice the following momentous factoid; the word awesome ends with "me." It could end with you but then it would be called "awesoyou," and that would just be weird.

Anyhoo… Here's what you've all been waiting for, the Awesome Alphabet. Apply it to your life and happy dance like you've never happy danced before people!

A: Am I awesome or what?

B: Believe it, I'm awesome.

C: Can't stop being awesome.

D: Do you want to be awesome like me; I know you do.

E: Everybody loves my awesomeness.

F: Forget mediocre, I'm awesome!

G: Gosh, can I really be this awesome? Yes I can.

H: Have you ever seen this much awesome before; now you have.

I: I'm having a nice day, because I'm awesome.

J: Just a reminder, wait for it, I'm awesome.

K: Keep reading this; it talks about me and awesome, which are the same.

L: Let's all take a moment and bask in my awesomeness.

M: Most of the time, I just sit around being awesome.

N: Never forget, you got to experience my awesomeness!

O: Oh my, I'm really awesome.

P: Please, please, take a picture of me being awesome, which I am, right now.

Q: Quiet is not necessary to hear me being awesome. I have loud awesomeness.

R: Remind me to tell you about how awesome I am, because I will.

S: Seriously, I am this awesome.

T: Total Awesomeness Right Here People!

U: Under all circumstances, I'm awesome.

V: Very few people are this awesome, but I am.

W: With all this awesomeness comes great responsibility, to be awesome.

X: X? Uhm, I got nothin'.

Y: You have benefitted from my awesomeness. You're welcome.

Z: Zebras have stripes, airplanes have wings, I have awesome.

Now start dancing!

Section 2: Body Image (One size does not fit all.)

Put the fashion magazine down and slowly walk away. I think those girls need to eat something. If others aren't satisfied with your body, who cares? They aren't wearing it.

Being different from one another is what makes us interesting. As much as I think a planet full of people just like me would be a great idea, it probably would get boring after a couple thousand years, maybe.

Let's face it; if you look different you're probably going to hear about it. Being tall, short, fat, thin, this or that brings out the idiot in some people. They're not perfect (obviously by what they say about others) and no doubt have body image oddities they could work on.

If you truly want an aspect of your body to change, you have to change it. That's not very profound I know. If you're shorter or taller than you'd like, you're out of luck. If, however, you're fat or skinny (in your eyes) there's only about a bazillion ways you can work on that. You pick what seems right for you. You change it when it seems right to do so and you reap the rewards as you progress. Wow, a lot of "you" in there, get it?

Now for my disclaimer. I am not a doctor, psychiatrist, psychologist, dietician or certified personal trainer or body builder or gym rat or fitness coach or fitness know it all or fitness guru. What comes next is my catchy way of looking at food and fitness. That's all.

Make an appointment with any of the people I'm not to find out your specific nutritional and exercise dos and don'ts. Also, look deep into yourself for why and how you've reached your current situation.

Emotions can have a huge impact on eating habits and self-esteem. All the "eat right and exercise" propaganda is useless if your emotions and self-esteem are the core problem. Don't ignore it – seek help. There; now for my catchy way of saying things about what you eat and what makes you sweat.

Now for my other disclaimer. I'm about to use the terms fat and skinny. They aren't insults, they are terms. People who are overweight are carrying extra fat cells on their bodies and people who are underweight aren't carrying enough fat cells and, or muscle tissue. Of course, fat and skinny falls into the "eye of the beholder" category but the beholder's opinion doesn't count; the opinion of the one wearing the body counts. If you think you're fat or skinny, maybe the following will help.

A little too fat; eat a little less but do eat fresh, super healthy, natural foods and drink water as often as possible. Don't forget to exercise more and be consistent. A little too skinny; eat calorie rich (not fatty) foods, include fresh, super healthy, natural foods too and drink water as often as possible. Maybe work out with weights like a raving lunatic. Both should do lots of research on the Internet, consult a trainer, maybe join a gym and/or find others to do whatever it is you're going to do, but above all, get started.

Diet and Exercise: First, consult a doctor before doing anything you should consult a doctor before doing. If it grows out of the ground, eat it, preferably raw. At least don't cook it until it's nutritionally worthless or cover it in batter and deep fry it then smother it in butter and cream sauce. If it walks on the ground eat it once in a while. If it swims in the water (where else) or flies through the sky (where else) eat it more often than the walking entree. Eat to live rather than live to eat.

Cravings are a pain in the butt. Why do we always crave the very things we're not supposed to eat? Why can't we crave broccoli or rice cakes? Nope, we crave hot, gooey cheddar cheese sauce with a scant hint of a fraction of a part of a broccoli bit and rice cakes covered in donuts. When cravings hit (and they will) fight them with food. Say what? Fight them with the very thing they're about, food. Fight them with fruits and vegetables and water. Fight them with the nutrition fruits and vegetables provide. Things that grow out of the ground or from trees (which grow out of the ground by the way) could be looked at like natural nutritional "medicine."

Disclaimer number three here. I put quotations around the word medicine so no one will think I'm trying to diagnose anything or prescribe anything or circumvent the medical profession and the practice of medicine in any way, and stuff like that. When I used the word medicine, it was meant to give you a new way to look at these foods. They may not be the most glamorous things to chew on but they can do glorious things once inside you to better your overall health, help you lose weight, lower blood pressure and cholesterol and a host of other neat tricks. Of course, you should chit chat with an honest to goodness doctor type before and probably during any major or minor shift in your eating habits.

Exercise: If you don't like a certain part or parts of your body, make changes over time. Don't go on some fad or extreme program. Concentrate on what you feel needs work and dedicate more time to it than you have been. Set reasonable goals. Do the happy dance when you reach them. By the way, happy dancing is a form of exercise. Stay consistent. Make your version of working out a part of your life and work through the difficult parts. When you start, every part of exercising is a difficult part. It will get better - I said, it will get better.

So, what are you waiting for? You can read more of the book later – get going right now and start taking back control of your eating and exercise habits. You deserve it!

Section 3: The Real Us (Who are you now? Who do you want to be? What are the differences?)

We're all somebody right now, duh. We may not be the somebody we want to be though. If that's you, it might explain why you don't "feel yourself." If you don't feel yourself, ask whoever you happen to be right now who you truly want to be. Stop. Be careful here. If you can answer the "who do you want to be" question you've just begun the process of change.

After coming to grips with who you want to be, the next question is what are the differences between who you are now and the potential you of the future? Stop, careful time again. If you know the differences between the "now you" and the "future you," the "now you" can make plans to get you to the "future you." Cool, huh? These plans will cause a lot of changes. You may start eating right and exercising, go back to school, change jobs, move to a new city, state or country or even end a relationship that is hurting you. You may end up doing more than one of these at the same time. Now that's exciting.

You shouldn't look at these changes as the "I hate change" type of changes. Look at them as the "Oh my goodness, this is truly who I want to be" type changes. You've probably known it for a long time. You may have told yourself and your friends you're going to do this and going to do that but you've not really done anything substantial about it, until now. You deserve this because, well, just because you do since, you are awesome. (see *Section 1: "I like me and I agree"* for a full explanation of the "you are awesome" reference)

Now may be the perfect time for you to look deep inside yourself in the most honest way you can. What will you be looking for? You'll be looking for, you; the real you. You may not recognize yourself at first. That's Ok. Getting re-acquainted with yourself is a good thing. It won't take long before you'll be the best of friends with yourself again. The more acquainted with yourself you become, the more control you'll get back. More control equals more happiness. More happiness equals you enjoying being yourself again.

The changes you'll need to make to become more acquainted with yourself will require dedication and consistency. You'll no doubt face all kinds of reactions from those around you. Stay focused on your goal of becoming the real you. You deserve to be happy with yourself.

Section 4: Days, Weeks and Months (A great time for change.)

Most of the time, most people don't like most of the changes which take place in their lives. We like staying the way we are, after all, we've been doing things a certain way for a while and we're pretty good at it. But change can be a welcome thing if we don't like what or who we are right now. For many, who they are is often a manufactured image. Simply put, they dress and act like those around them because they have to or they won't be accepted. It's fun and cool at first but can get old. Eventually they'll want to change.

They may want to change because they're maturing or the group is changing and they don't want to change in the same way. Maybe they fear they won't be accepted anymore if they break out of the mold placed around them. They can't even figure out how to explain the change to the group if they were to move in their own direction. They still want to be friends but not a cookie cut out of others. They want to make the change in a way it's uninterrupted and the pressure to go back won't be in their face. They need to find the proper time for the change. That time is called, at a minimum, the week end. Other time frames such as Thanksgiving break, Christmas and New Year's breaks and spring break are good too. The big one, of course, is summer break (if you're in school). It could be a vacation if you're not.

These times can be used to make the changes they want without interruption. All I'm saying is; they need time to themselves to think about what they really want and then to do it. So how do they explain the change? Simple, they just say the name of the time off. An example would be, "Hey, what happened to you?" Answer; summer break. That's it. Nothing else is needed. Ok, if a profound explanation is requested they can give them this; "It was time for a change." After all, that's the most honest answer they can give.

I met a kid named Shawn at the end of his sophomore year who is a perfect example of what I'm saying. He's proof it works.

He was sitting at his usual spot outside the school waiting for the bus to take him home. He was wearing a costume; every piece of clothing was black (not that there's anything wrong with that), his natural medium brown hair was died coal black. He was wearing about 20 bracelets, earrings which looked like daggers, and various other attention getters. He said nothing, ever. So, I decided to talk to him. It started slow and easy like, "Hey" or "Did you feed your brain today?" That's my way of asking students if they've learned something. After a while we started talking to each other.

I found out he wasn't happy. I told him he didn't look happy but didn't know if it was an act to keep people away or a true statement of his emotions. I see kids all the time who come across as being happy to the point of needing sedation, then being under the weight of the world in a complete state of despair, then back to happyville. All this happens in the same day. Most of it is simply fake steak and phony bologna. He wasn't faking anything.

He wasn't what he seemed to be. He portrayed himself as a gothic kid or "goth" and had from about seventh grade. As far as I could tell, his version of being goth consisted of the black clothing and accessories and hanging around other kids wearing the same type stuff. Some goth kids in my study hall would talk about their belief in vampires, the benefits of an anarchist styled government system, how much they hated their parents and how misunderstood they all felt. He spent his sophomore year not wanting to be goth but unable to get away because of his "friends," you know, the people who probably wouldn't understand or tolerate him "ungothing" himself. He worried that if he changed, he'd have no friends at all. That might be worse than staying where he was, or so he thought.

I asked him whose opinion of him was more important, his own or others. He said his own. I asked him if the reason he hadn't made the change yet was due to being in school around his friends every day. He said it was. I asked him why he wanted to change (after all, he had changed into a goth from whatever he was before). He said being goth had run its course, it didn't feel right and he felt depressed because he couldn't be himself. He had things he wanted to try and felt trapped inside himself.

I asked him if he were moving to another school for the next year would he go there as a goth. He said no. The school year was almost over. I told him there was no reason for him to return to this one as a goth either. He was only a couple weeks away from beginning the ungothing process. He was also only a couple months away from revealing the person he truly was to everyone in school once the new school year had started. He was about to enter "the summer break zone."

When I explained to him how it works, he smiled. He smiled! He started making plans right then. We talked about his plans and concerns about being made fun of or not being taken seriously. He was ready. Summer break came and went. He returned to school a different kid.

He actually looked taller. He hadn't gown, as far as I knew, but he was standing up straighter; it happens when you're happy. His hair was the color it grew out of his skull for the first time in four years. He wore different t-shirts (some black) or hoodies and jeans with holes strategically placed for the fashionable teen. Tennis shoes were a must. In fact, he had really cool shoes, running shoes, expensive, multicolored running shoes. He fit right in with 90% of the kids.

Before long he was talking with other kids and seemed just fine. He began waiting for a bus after school again and we talked. Actually, he talked, a lot. He talked about all the changes he had made and how good he felt. He never really mentioned his former friends; some of them still liked him but most ignored him. He didn't care. He was himself.

He tried out for the cross-country team. What? Since when do you run, I asked? He said, since now. Good answer. He made it and even competed in the Sectional meet. Being on the cross-country team meant he had to wear their t-shirts and hoodie now and then. He went out and bought other school shirts and wore them all the time. He wore the school's colors, neon colors, tie dye and anything else he, I repeat, he, wanted to. He began to be identified by other kids and his teachers as a really good guy to be around.

His senior year went along in the same way as his junior year had. He'd say hi to me in the hallway with a great big smile on his face. I think he started dating too, hence the smile. To prove my point, I want you to read, very carefully, the last portion of this story.

He's graduated now and assists the cross country and track coaches. We even ran a mile together a couple weeks back. He told me he remembers the kid he used to be; mad, confused and depressed. He told me he's so glad he made the changes he did. I told him I was proud of him and that he was, and still is, an example for other kids to follow. He smiled.

Listen to this. By the end of his senior year he was a pretty popular guy with lots of friends. When the votes were counted for senior stand outs to be included in the yearbook, he was voted, and is very proud of the title, "Most Changed."

Shawn and I in 2016.

Section 5: Stand Your Ground - (Believe me, your beliefs are worth believing. Believe it.)

Here's a delicate one - or is it? I don't think it should be. After all, I'm entitled to my beliefs about, absolutely everything. I think we should be able to talk openly about, absolutely everything. It used to be, people said you shouldn't talk about religion or politics. If we don't talk about them, how can we evaluate our elected officials and the political party (if any) they represent. How would we spread our religious beliefs (if any) if we didn't yack about them once in a while? We need to talk and express our beliefs about, absolutely everything. Believe it or not, expressing yourself can boost your self-esteem. I'll give my beliefs about some stuff in a minute.

First, I want to explain the obvious. You are entitled to your beliefs about, absolutely everything. You can believe what you want, about what you want, whenever and wherever you want. You should have control over your beliefs and the freedom to change your mind about them as you please. I stand by my beliefs no matter what. That is until I'm convinced there's a better way. At that point, I'll stand by my new beliefs as strongly as I stood for my previous ones. I'm not confused or waffling like some politicians are guilty of doing. I simply determine the new information is credible and accurate and I need to change my mind. I'm happy to do so because no one has changed my mind for me. The person talking to me has given me things to think about. I think about them and make my decision. I'm in control. That's a good feeling. Actually, you always have control over your beliefs since they're inside you. You can't always express them or act on them if someone has control over you. That control must be yours again if you ever want to properly and proudly stand up for your beliefs.

Here are some of mine, but first, my disclaimer; I have found it impossible during my life here on earth to agree with absolutely everything I've ever seen or heard. Therefore, there are some things I disagree with. In fact, everything I agree with has the direct result of me disagreeing with the opposite position and vice versa. Just because I disagree with something doesn't mean I'm using "hate speech." It means, I - do not – agree. It goes no deeper than that.

Some of my beliefs are as follows; I'm a Christian and believe in creation. I don't think my ancestors came from apes or anything else. I find it hard to grasp that fossil remains of a creature dating back 50 million years will be found; then fossils of a similar creature, that supposedly lived 10 million years later will be found and it's supposed to be the evolutionary kin to the first one. This is determined because, let's say, it doesn't have a tail, which clearly explains, something or other. Ok then, where are all the fossils for the countless millions of "in between" creatures with different length tails? You'd think you could find a lot of them, not just the long tail version and the no tail version. Couldn't the two creatures simply be two different but similar animals having always been that way? There are many dog breeds. Some look similar and some are very different. They're still dogs.

I believe in the "big bang" theory too, really I do. I believe the big bang went something like this; a long time ago, God decided he wanted to make stuff, planets, trees, stars, mallard ducks and so on. He told everyone in heaven to stand back and BANG, it happened. No doubt, creating the universe made a lot of racket. I mean, you can't do that sort of thing quietly can you?

Since I'm a Christian, I believe in Christ. I believe Jesus was a real man, a Jewish carpenter by trade then a traveling teacher, preacher and healer before he allowed himself to be killed on the cross. I believe he was the savior of mankind and I am his child. I'm going to live forever in heaven with Him (He's there now – His tomb is empty – you can go look if you want – you won't find Him). I believe Jesus was and is, the Son of God.

I believe freedom is worth fighting and dying for. I believe the men and women who serve our country in the Armed Forces are heroes. Jesus told us the greatest love of all is demonstrated when one person lays down their life for a friend. The exact quote is in the book of John: chapter 15, verse 13.

I believe those who commit crimes should be imprisoned. I believe having more prisons would employ many people on the short term to build them, employ many people on the long term to work them, and of course, house more prisoners. No more overcrowding and no early release because of it. I believe I have the right to protect myself, my loved ones and others against violent people (who should be in one of the new prisons).

I believe in adoption. Children need a home where they will be loved and cared for. I believe in loving with all your heart, soul, mind and strength (the wisest of all men said that). I believe my wife is the most extraordinary person on earth. I haven't met everyone yet, but I stand by my belief.

By the way, you don't have to agree with me. In fact, you can be vehemently opposed to everything I stand for and every word in this book. Stand your ground.

Section 6: Self-Improvement Made "Easy" (A little at a time and nothing is off limits)

Very few of us are completely satisfied with ourselves. We want to be thinner, have more hair (not me), make more money (me) and lower our cholesterol. Things are the way they are and will stay that way unless we do something about them. Notice I didn't say we should do a complete turnaround, perform a profound and life altering rejuvenation of our present condition, blah, blah, blah. Nope. I said "something." It doesn't have to be big. It just has to be. It has to take place and you are the perfect person to make it happen. Again, YOU are the perfect person to MAKE IT HAPPEN.

Self-improvement is a tricky thing it seems. Experts of all kinds claim to have the best way for you to improve yourself.

When I started seriously looking into my own self-improvement I had questions. These questions usually started with the word how, as in, how exactly do I move out, over, under or through the barriers to my happiness and success? After listening to many people and reading enough text to cover the Great Plains, I realized something. It all sounded good, but still left the "how" dilemma in place. I couldn't figure out how to make huge changes in my life but felt I could make small ones, then, see how far they'd take me. As it turns out, they've taken me pretty far and I'm not done yet.

So, what to do first and how? I decided to make changes maybe only I'd notice and do it the turtle's way, you know, slow and steady. I could handle that. I didn't want to jump too far into something, spend a bunch of money (because I didn't have any to spare), go to any week long, week end, day long or afternoon seminars (again, no money or time). I had to do it myself. I also decided that if a modest change was good enough for one area of my life, maybe it was good for two or three. I knew it would take effort, real effort, to start and stay with it. I never have been able to wrap my mind around the concepts of willing things to happen or visualizing something and it will come to pass. I've visualized a lot of things in my life and I'm still not an astronaut and my house isn't located on my own private island; so much for visualization.

My first change was to get healthier. Since "getting healthier" was too broad an area, I focused on exercise. I really didn't like the idea but knew it was necessary. I've never had a weight problem (6'3" and 180 lbs.) but I've also never been too muscular. A fast metabolism and skinny DNA I guess. I started doing push-ups and sit ups in the mornings before my shower; Monday, Wednesday and Friday were push-ups with sit ups on Tuesday and Thursday. The next week I'd alternate. I took the week ends off. I couldn't do a lot at first but I was doing them consistently.

As days passed they got easier and I was doing more. That's what I wanted. I began feeling a wee bit happier about myself. Not overwhelming euphoria, just wee happiness. It was enough to make me set goals. For push-ups it was three sets until I face planted the floor. I'd be able to do about twenty for the first set, then fifteen, then whatever I could do for the last set before tasting carpet. For sit ups, the number was anything near one hundred. That came easier for me but still hurt later that day.

I continued with the occasional extra day off due to medical conditions known as, "man, I'm tired," "I feel like crap" and remembering I hadn't done them until after I was showered and dressed. I didn't worry about it since I knew it was just one of those things. I got right back to it the next morning. In a couple months, yes months, I felt a lot better.

Three things happened about that time. One, I noticed a growth on my chest. It was the shadow of what I believed to be muscle. Pectoral muscles or "pecs" I think they're called. I also saw similar growth on my shoulders and arms. My abs (a one pack) were now definitely a one and a half pack. Two, someone at work said the magic words, to wit, "looks like you've been working out." I told them what I was doing and they said "well, it's working." Bless their heart. Three, I went home and decided to start lifting weights. My decision made me happier. It didn't freak me out. I actually wanted to start.

I consulted my slightly older and much bigger brother Sam, his wife Alma and their son Matt about lifting. You see, my bro is 6'7" tall and began lifting in high school. He's never stopped. He's big. Yes, big, big, big. Alma was a star athlete at the U.S. Military Academy at West Point. She set records there and has a memorial at the academy for her achievements. She's also a member of the Tennessee High School Athletic Hall of Fame. Matt is 6' 3" like me but can bench press over 450 pounds. Really, I've seen it. It's humbling to say the least.

Anyway, I talked to them and got some pointers. I didn't have a lot of time or a partner to lift with. I was on my own. I began. It hurt. I was disappointed with what little weight I could lift. I decided I didn't like lifting weights. I kept lifting anyway. It got better.

Ultimately, the same thing happened with the weights that happened with the push-ups and sit ups. It got easier and I started lifting more. The time frame from the first push-up to the first bench press was about five months. Turtle, remember. It worked well. No rush, but I had moved from two basic exercises in my bedroom to eight or so in a gym and it felt natural. I'd finish lifting (chest, back, shoulders, arms, neck) then do a hundred sit ups and run a mile. The mile took up to fourteen minutes if I felt like crap that day. My usual is nine and a half minutes.

There you go. That's it. I still do this type of work out today. It's treated me well. For a change I'll do a bunch of elbow to knee crunches while in the up push up position. They don't look like fun and they really aren't. No, that's not a typo – its sarcasm. Sometimes I'll hammer out one hundred push-ups from sets of 5, 10, 15, 20, 20, 15, 10 and 5. Variety is the spice of life after all (so is garlic, lots and lots of garlic).

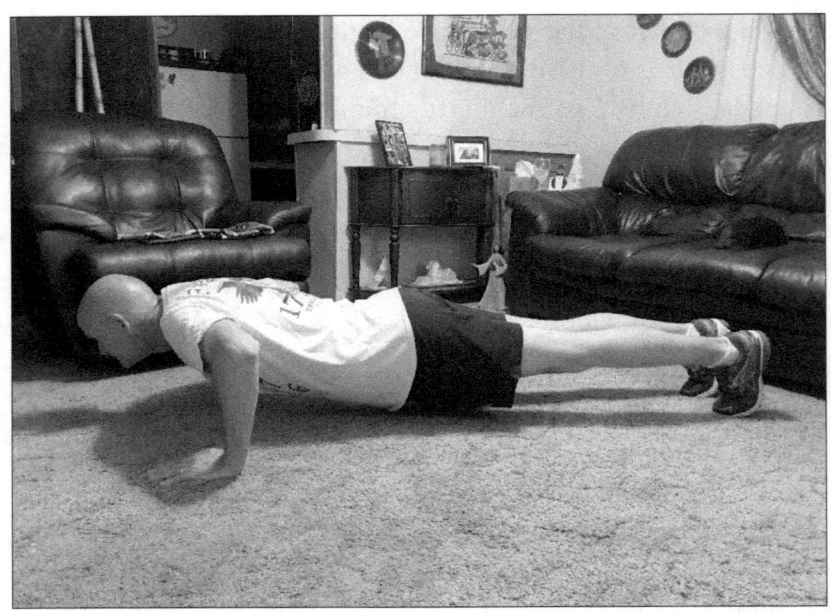

Heading for 100 pushups (total that is) in my home gym, aka, our living room. Not too bad for being in my 50s.

My next change needed to be my diet. I tried to eat healthier but found it takes a lot of money to eat a lot of healthy food. I did what I could. Then, it happened. I was put in a position where I had no choice but to eat better. It was out of my hands and into the hands of, my wife. Yep, after Cathy and I got married I started eating better, much better.

Cathy is a fantastic cook. She knows how to incorporate stuff like plants, which I never imagined eating, into our meals. Almost everything of the plant variety she's made for me hasn't been nearly as nasty as I had dreamed. All kidding aside, green stuff isn't bad. I don't jump for joy over it but I eat it because it tastes good-ish, it's good for me, and most of all, because Cathy has made it for me. I even choose to put things like spinach on my salad, not much, but it's there. That's an improvement and that's what it's all about.

There have been other changes which have made my happy meter take flight. I like painting. I've done many projects but most of them are given to other people or organizations. Cathy and I both got a boost when she picked out new colors for the living room, spare bathroom, kitchen walls and cabinets. I painted them. Of course, new furniture and decorations were next. After all, we had changed the feel of those rooms and everything had to match. No, that's not self-improvement, its home improvement but improvement all the same. Cathy loves the new look and that makes me happy. I worked hard on it and it turned out really well and that makes me happy. It no longer smells like paint and that makes me happy. You get the idea.

I changed my look. I was cursed with fine hair. Not fine as in good, but fine as in so wimpy if a person sneezed in another room, my hair moved. I developed a circular bare spot at the top of my head a few years back. No one could really see it if I remained standing but I had to sit sometimes. Male Pattern Baldness, who thought up that idea?

I used to cut my hair really short (high and tight style – consult a US Marine if you want to know what that is) for Color Guard use but it looked like a horse shoe with a shiny bald spot in the middle. After Cathy and I got married she convinced me to shave my entire head bald. I had tried it the summer before we started seeing each other but it didn't look right. Once again, I shaved myself into a walking Q-ball and strolled into the living room. Cathy was on the phone. She looked at me, nearly dropped the phone and said she loved it. I've been happily bald ever since.

I've even learned to swim - rather ungracefully. My version of swimming is vigorously beating the water (and the occasional passerby) while maneuvering about the pool. Cathy is an expert swimmer. She's helped me deal with the awkwardness I bring to the pool and now I look forward to going. I never felt that way before. I also get to see her in a bathing suit. Bonus Points!

I'm not going to lie (of course) it took some time to do this on the turtle schedule. There's nothing wrong with that. After all, I have a job and responsibilities not a million bucks a dietician and a personal trainer. However, in that time I have built muscles, eat healthier and look better, according to Cathy, and she's the only one who matters. I'm trying new things and I have a positive outlook on life and the future. I think that qualifies as self-improvement.

Your self-improvement can be anything you want it to be. You decide what needs improvement, do research on the best way to achieve your goals then decide when to start. This is big – none of the thinking, planning, wishing, hoping, or any other preparatory things you do will amount to anything if you don't start. You must begin your self-improvement journey at some point. Maybe, just maybe – the time is now!

Section 7: Rocky Balboa's Hard-Hitting Wisdom (Sandra' story)

Good 'ol Rocky once said it isn't how hard a person can get hit that matters but how hard they can get hit and keep moving forward. Coming from a boxer, even a make believe one, it makes sense. How about us?

We've all known people who have been "hit." They've been hit by problems with their health, finances, families, personal stuff and the general crap-olla we all face. Some break down under the weight. Some get through it but are changed. Some get through it and don't change at all. Then there are the rare few who come through it stronger than they were before. Our daughter Sandra is one of those rare few.

I met Sandra at the end of her freshman year in high school. She tried out for the Color Guard and made it. It was clear she had self-confidence and was pretty much fearless.

Once in the Color Guard her sense of humor came out. She could be perfectly serious while performing, but as soon as the performance was over and we were safely tucked away in our prep room, she'd bust up laughing about something she found funny during the performance. We'd all start laughing too but wouldn't understand why. She'd explain it, we wouldn't get it and she'd bust up laughing about that.

As Sandra increased in knowledge and rank, her leadership skills became obvious. She knew her stuff and could teach others. I decided to start a Drill Instructor program within the Color Guard using its members as my assistants. Sandra was in the first class of Drill Instructor graduates. She was very, very good. She was impressive. She was intimidating. Some of her former recruits still have nightmares about her. One of her first recruits was my future step son, Luke. He became a Drill Instructor too.

Sandra remained a Drill Instructor throughout her time in the Color Guard eventually attaining the rank of Lieutenant. She set the bar so high; the record she set for total awards earned wasn't broken for five years.

Something else happened during Sandra's time in the Color Guard; I got to know her not only as her coach but as a mentor. This is a normal situation between coaches and some students. Sandra needed someone to talk to and receive advice from. She talked. I listened and gave what advice I could. She thanked me and went on her way. That's how it was for quite a while.

Sandra needed someone to talk to and advice because she didn't have that at home; at all. I'm not going to go into what her home life was like except to say, it drove her to seek adult counsel elsewhere. I'm glad she chose me.

Mid-way through her senior year, things at home got so bad Sandra had to move out. She moved in with various families of Color Guard kids but none lasted very long; not because of her. As a last resort, Sandra began living in her truck. She ate cold Ramen Noodles and un-microwaved instant oatmeal packets and showered in the high school's girl's locker room early in the morning so as not to be caught. Her parents (Dad and Step Mom – Mom and Step Dad) moved to two different states leaving her behind.

While living in her truck, she kept going to school, getting good grades, working and performing with the Color Guard. She didn't tell anyone. When it was discovered, something had to be done. Sandra had bonded with my future wife Cathy. Cathy is Luke's mom and never, I mean never, missed a Color Guard performance. I think Sandra picked up on the kind of woman and mother Cathy was then and still is.

Cathy took educational guardianship of Sandra and Sandra moved in with her. Sandra and Cathy hit it off perfectly. Cathy treated Sandra like her own daughter. Sandra was given her own room (something she had never had). It had a bed in it (also something she had never had). Get the picture I'm painting here? They were like sisters. Then, they became like mother and daughter and eventually loved each other in the same way. Sandra was happy, Cathy was happy, and I was happy Sandra had found a real home.

Cathy and I would talk to Sandra about anything on her mind, like her future. She wanted to join the military. That was cool. She wanted to do more with her art; cool too. Cathy and I took our responsibilities of helping Sandra very seriously and she appreciated it.

I was given a great honor when Sandra asked me to escort her onto the gym floor during the Senior Night Honors Program for the Color Guard. That privilege is usually reserved for parents. I was so proud.

My two girls, Cathy and Sandra.

Sandra graduated with honors from the National Art Honor Society and began her journey toward the Air Force, like I had. She chose to be a cop, like I had. Cathy and I alternated taking her to appointments with her recruiter and other places. I took her to the range and taught her the fundamentals of shooting.

This was Sandra's senior night recognition ceremony at a home basketball game. Her Color Guard achievements and future goals were read over the loud speaker to the crowd. Unlike so many students who have goals for their future but never achieve them, Sandra's determination to get up and keep moving forward when she got knocked down by circumstances and disappointments ensured she achieved hers – and much more.

I took Sandra to a couple shooting ranges to teach her the basics before she enlisted in the USAF. She was pretty good from the start and only got better from there.

We had a blast (pun intended). She's now an Air Force expert marksman with both pistol and rifle.

By that time Sandra was calling Cathy "the mom," me "the dad" and herself "the kid." We even had t-shirts made. Then, it happened; I was taking Sandra to see her recruiter and she handed me a picture. It was her at graduation. On the back she wrote the following;

For My Dad; On June 6, 2009 I accomplished a goal to graduate from JCHS. I would never have been able to make it through all of the "interesting" situations without you there to support me, guide me and motivate me. You know I'm not good with words or emotions. But I do know I love you just like any kid loves their real dad. Thank you so much. Love, Sandra "The Kid"

I loved her, too, as something I had never been, a dad. She told me it was how she felt and not to make a big deal about it. I told her I loved her too. We laughed a little (I think she punched me in the arm) and went on to her appointment.

Sandra is an example to others of goal setting and persistence. She's also an example of what can happen when you let your heart try again. Sandra allowed us into her life and now we're a family. Sandra is not blood related to either of us but we're still a family. Cathy and I got married a year and a half after she joined the Air Force but we're still a family. We're a family because we consider each other part of ourselves.

Sandra not only overcame the hardships and neglect of her youth, she excelled. She had decided years before not to end up like those around her. She would be better. She didn't trust very easily and it took time for her to realize Cathy and I were with her to stay. She's independent, intelligent, beautiful and successful. She's all the things she shouldn't be when you think of what she had to endure.

I'm as proud as a dad can be to tell you, this kid who I met with the black clothes and tipped hair in the spring of 2005, is my daughter and an American Airman just like she wanted. She's come a long way since living in her truck. She is (as of this writing) a United States Air Force Security Forces Staff Sergeant Military Working Dog Handler stationed in New Mexico. She's there with her husband, Daniel. She's also been stationed in Greenland, Washington D.C., Virginia, Japan and is an Afghanistan veteran. That's my girl!

I had never been referred to as "dad" until Sandra came along. I had to get used to hearing it since that name had always been directed at someone else up to that point in my life. When I hear her say it, it makes me profoundly happy. Yeah, the t-shirts are a little silly, but speaking as a dad, I think they're pretty cool. (see what I did there?)

Sandra at Thule AFB, Greenland. Thule is where Santa Claus is tracked each Christmas Eve on his trip around the world. It was Sandra's first base after graduating from basic training and the USAF Security Forces Academy.

After Sandra graduated from Military Working Dog school she was given Ajo as her first K9 partner. As you can see, Ajo can be all business. When he could no longer serve the military, Sandra was allowed to adopt him as a pet. He's all rest and relaxation now – as it should be.

Sandra messing with the chalkboard in my classroom again. You could say, it was a premonition. I'm glad it came true.

Sandra said a million times she'd never get married. She wanted to focus on her career and didn't want any "distractions" or other commitments. Nope. Not going to happen. I'd like you to meet her husband, Daniel.

Section 8: Rambo's Motivation (What's your something?)

John J. Rambo, the fictional former Green Beret Vietnam veteran was man of few words, a lot of grunts and yells, but few actual words. However, in the last of the movies starring this human war machine he told a mercenary for hire, "Live for nothing or die for something." I like that a whole bunch.

I don't want to live for nothing. I want my life to have meaning. I want my life to have been about something, many things as a matter of fact. I've been around for a while now and I'm just not done. I'm writing this book because I'm not done. I want to help others because I'm not done. These are some of the things I want my life to be about. You can read about the other things in the "Me" topic of this book.

As for you, what is your life about? What defines you? Why do you get up in the morning? What are you trying to accomplish? The most basic answer is "something," but what? This is not a tough thing to answer if you're honest with yourself. What is your top personal priority? Better yet, what are your top three personal priorities? They may be the very things you've lost control of but also the things you want to base your life around. If they're your true priorities and you're not living your life around them – you're living a lie. You think and feel one thing and do another. It's like being an enemy of your own self. This is not cool people. You deserve better.

A change is in order. Each of us has to identify our core, our true self, our inner being thing or whatever it is which will make us say, hey, that's the me I've been looking for. Being totally honest with yourself can be a little difficult but it's necessary. You'll have to ask yourself direct questions and give direct answers. Don't pull any punches. You may want to punch yourself when you're done, though. No subject is off limits. That would be cheating.

Since living for nothing is out of the question, what are the questions to ask? I already covered some but here are some more. Am I living my life according to my priorities or someone else's rules? If it's the latter, who are they and why am I following them? Have I achieved the goals I set for myself at this point in my life? If not, what has prevented it?

Do I feel fulfilled spiritually, emotionally, physically and financially? If not, what has prevented it?

Many times, the major reason we aren't who, or where we want in life, is due to other people. These people have personal relationships with us to whatever degree. At worse, they may be living for the sole purpose of pleasing themselves at our expense. At best, they're just unaware we have different priorities and goals. They won't figure it out on their own, we have to enlighten them.

You may not like some of the answers you give yourself, then again, you just might. You might like some of them because they re-affirm you've been doing things right. You may come to the revelation you're not directly responsible for not achieving this or that goal by now. It might hit you that the solution(s) aren't as huge and horrible as you thought they would be. You just might see things much more clearly after your personal interrogation session. Removing the barriers may be so doable you start doing them right away, getting rid of the garbage that's prevented your life from having things worth living for. Ask the questions, give the answers, remove the garbage and start living your life for the things you want.

If you are indeed living your personal priorities, you have built in motivation. Not just for each new day but for the future. You can expand on these priorities and possibly influence others. Your life is and can continue to be good. How cool is that? It's really, really cool.

As for me, it's simple. I live my life for Christ, my wife, family and those I can help. I am a Christian, husband, father, grandfather, son, brother, uncle, friend, coach, mentor, instructor, speaker, author and a snappy dresser (according to my wife). I live for these people and my life is good. I hope you'll join me.

Section 9: A way to like exercise (It sounds crazy I know)

I'll get straight to the point. Liking exercise is very difficult if you don't like physical exertion, sweat or spending time in a gym or on your machine at home or in your living room with the furniture moved out of the way so you can try to keep up with the oh so happy and already in shape jazzorific, beautiful body, aerobidance instructor.

I tell people the same thing all the time. It's not an undiscovered truth or revelation but it seems to help them look at whatever they're doing in the category of exercise in a new and likeable way. I'll use 20 push-ups as an example. When you've finished 20 push-ups you are 20 push-ups stronger than you've ever been in your life. This, of course, is not based on science or physiology or any of that stuff. This is an outlook.

Look at exercise in such a way you're convinced it always helps you. Be 20 push-ups stronger by doing 20 push-ups. Be a half mile better by running or jogging or walking, maybe crawling or being rolled a half mile away from where you start. Whatever it is you do when you do exercise, look at it as making an improvement in your life. Control your outlook about exercise and it could go from, I have to exercise, to, I get to exercise, to, I'm going to go make myself better.

Chapter 2: Parenting 101

Section 1: Young Children (Basic Training)

You are their parent so act like it. You are automatically their friend. You love them and they love you, the learning process can't stop that. If they don't learn how to behave now, their behavior later may shred your nerves, interfere with your ability to go out as a family, bankrupt your finances, ruin your vacations, destroy your vehicles, evaporate your credit rating, rupture your family's reputation and so much more.

It's really never too early to establish rules of behavior but you must be consistent or you're wasting your time. A lack of diligence on your part will be exploited by your bundle of joy whenever possible. It's a natural thing for kids to push the boundaries. Of course, there needs to be, scratch that, there must be boundaries in the first place. It shows you care. It's a lot of hard work but you'll be thankful in the end.

Never ask your young child to decide something you should decide for them. Example; let's say you're at the grandparent's house or in the toy aisle of a store; you approach your child and ask, "Do you want to go?" Their response will be screaming and flailing, tears and shouts of anguish all resounding in the answer, "no." When it's time to go, it's time to go, don't ask, don't beg, just go. Yeah, I know, they'll still flail but it beats asking a small child a question you already know the answer to. It also gets the kid used to not having a say in matters in which they have no say. The older kids get the more "say" they have. During their birthdays they have all the say, of course. Point; if you don't want the flail to begin, don't go near the toy aisle unless you have every intention of buying a toy. Never beg your two-foot-tall offspring for anything.

Stop the baby talk once they're no longer an actual baby and potty train ASAP. Require them to use words to tell you what they want. Our granddaughter started putting words together as itty bitty sentence before she was two. When she was two, she could ask for what she wanted and say things like, "Oh,

Does this look right to you?

Grandma, I love your shoes." A few months later she was saying multiple small sentences with voice inflections, facial expressions and the occasional hands on her hips display for a higher diva rating.

I've been around kids up to four years old who still grunt for their food, point at what they want, fill their diapers, suck on pacifiers and crawl almost everywhere they go. Give me a break. You'd think the parents would want their child to advance. These things are cute for only so long; 36 months is too long.

Section 2: Respect (No one dies from saying Sir, Ma'am, please and thank you.)

When I interviewed to be the study hall supervisor at Jennings County High School, the principal at the time told me what study hall had been like the previous five years; in a word, horrible. I sat in disbelief as he described what some of the students did in class and to the teachers. By the way; not a single teacher had returned for a second year in that time. He said study hall students were a constant disciplinary problem for him, the assistant principals and the guidance counselors. Yes, I said constant, as in every day, sometimes every period of the day. Are you kidding me? He wasn't.

The teacher before me would have a bell on his desk like the ones you ring for service at a counter. He'd "ding" it to let the class know they were being too loud; not a bad idea, actually. After the kids stole five of them, he stopped bringing them in; not a bad idea either. He was duct taped to his chair. It started as a joke. The duct tape laden boys acted like they were doing it and they were. Paper wads flew everywhere, many in the class were asleep, even lying on the floor and no work got done. There's more but I'm sure you get the gruesome picture.

It wasn't a matter of no control over the class it was a matter of where the control came from. Hint: The kids had it. The teachers would write the kids up and send them to the office. The principals would administer whatever disciplinary control was deemed necessary and the kid would behave better but only for a while. While they were behaving better, another kid would take their place as the resident moron. It was a cycle that had to stop, and I was next in line to try.

The principal told me something I actually disputed during my interview. He said there were all kinds of different kids in study hall and a lot of them (sometimes over 100). He said I'd have to deal with all of them. Here's my dispute. I said; "No Sir, I won't have to deal with them, they'll have to deal with me." He said, "You're hired."

It wouldn't be a cake walk but I was determined to take control of the class away from the disorderly mob and I did. I accomplished this in short order by injecting respect into all who entered my classroom, respect for the school, me and each other. I would have it no other way. After the first report cards came out, an assistant principal told me he was asked something he hadn't been asked for in a long time. He said a female student asked him to have her schedule changed to be in my study hall. She said a friend of hers was in it and described it as a place a lot of work could get done. It was that way because I had control.

The principals had certain requirements for study hall. Students could do school work (duh) or read. If they didn't have work, they had to read. If they had work and got it done before the class ended, they had to read. If they had work and just didn't want to do it, cool, they had to read. It worked really well. The students chose what they did and both are educational.

Along with the Principal I required things too. These are some of the reasons I maintained control in my classes even though I was terribly outnumbered by teenagers.

1) Kids could call me Mr. Hulse or Sir; not hey you, baldy, old man, dude, bud, cool breeze, etc.

2) Kids who had passes to leave class would place their passes on my desk or hand them to me not throw them on my desk. Kids did that before my reputation began to precede me. I tore those passes up, moved their assigned seat to the table directly in front of my desk and refused to accept any passes from them for two weeks. An apology (sometimes written) was required of course. No kid treated me like they may have treated their parents. They conducted themselves to my liking, not their own.

3) If a student was talking to me, all others needing to do the same waited their turn. If they interrupt, they sat down; I might have gotten to them, eventually.

4) If it was "free time," which generally was the last ten minutes of class, they were allowed to move about the room, talk, listen to their music and such. If my phone rang, the class shushed themselves, usually after I perform the first shush, because, hey, I'm on the phone.

5) No matter what was going on (passes, questions, going to lunch, etc.) ladies went first. If nine boys were next in line to see me and one girl approaches, the girl went to the front of the line. It may seem like cutting in line but I was trying to teach manners to the boys and appreciation to the girls. It worked. The boys told each other to move out of the way or offered their place in line; I didn't have to say a word. The girls really liked it, not because they got to go first, but because it made them feel special.

Here's a good one; a girl would be in the back of the room with all the boys crowded in a mass in front of her; It's lunch time and the rest of the girls were at the door. I'd say "make a hole" and the boys would open a path for her straight to the door. Kind of impressive. No one griped because that was standard operating procedure in Mr. Hulse's study hall.

6) I heard "please" some of the time but I heard "Thank you" almost every time I signed a pass or let one kid work with another. When I signed a pass for a kid and handed it back to them, I'd sometimes not let go unless they said, "Thank you." Sometimes they looked at me with a blank stare or a look of slight panic, then realize what was missing and said, "Thank you," usually followed by, "I'm sorry." I'd grin, let go of the pass and they were on their way; again, no gripes.

7) When I had to say something to the whole class, I'd say "May I have your attention?" in a game show announcer voice. Everyone stopped what they were doing and looked at me. When I spoke, they listen. When they spoke, I listen. It's was a two-way street.

8) I told each class something the first day of school which probably did the most good in setting the proper tone. I told them to leave their attitudes at the door, I wouldn't tolerate them. If they were upset, ticked off, enraged, sick, tired, constipated or anything else that had fractured their mood, they needed to tell me so I'd have a clue. I'd do whatever I could to help but I couldn't help if I was kept in the dark. Throwing a *tude* at me later would only result in doom on them. The kids seemed to respect this policy. If they were having a bad day, I'd do what I could, if anything. If they treated me as if I was the cause of all their woes when I wasn't, I added to their woes.

It may sound like I was some ego maniac with a serious need to intimidate the youth of America. No. I just had a quiet class where work got done, kids got help and respect was shown for all, all the time. There was no other way; again, I wouldn't allow it.

Section 3: Parenting (A verb - A contact sport never requiring a computer.)

As parents, if anyone knows what's going on with your kid, you should. At least, you should always be trying. I'm not naïve; a parent knowing everything that goes on with their kid is the same as unicorns and a balanced federal budget – a fantasy. So how do you keep trying - by contact with your kid; a lot of contact. Talking with them is good. Talk about whatever is on their minds. It doesn't have to be a major subject. It can actually be trivial but if it's on their mind it's real and it's important. No matter what it is, talking about it is a way to maintain contact. They talk to their friends all the time about who knows what. They can carry on conversations about big, small and microscopic topics for 50 hours straight, as long as they have enough battery life. You may not want, or be able, to convers for that many hours (in a row) but convers about anything and everything. Hey, that sounds a lot like *Facebook*. *Facebook* is on the computer. You aren't a computer but you can imitate one and spend time with your kids getting to know what they're thinking, fearing, wanting, needing and so on. Let's face it, they don't need *Facebook* in front of their face, they need your face in front of their face.

Speaking of *Facebook* and any other mode of Internet personality posturing; you, the parent, may look at, inspect and extinguish the *Facebook* account your child uses whenever you want. You have my permission. That goes for their cell phones, iPads and anything else I've missed.

Parents used to worry about putting computers in their kid's rooms. Let's see now, the entire computerized world at my kid's fingertips in the privacy of their very own room with the door shut. Yep, worry would be the appropriate response. Why a parent would allow this is beyond me; the temptations to look at freaky, vulgar, profane, violent, sexual, disturbing, cruel and unusual subject matter is too great. It actually pops up on the screen for crying out loud. Pop! Filth! Temptation, temptation, temptation. Hey kid, do your homework instead. Good luck with that one.

Nowadays, their phones and practically everything else they have can be used as a worldwide filth, predator and harassment exposure device. You can and should monitor them, put filters on them and anything else you feel is necessary to maintain control and the best understanding of what your kid is seeing; but above all, you need to be there for them. Your kids have questions and will search anywhere for an answer. You must answer their questions not the rest of the world. The World Wide Web is no substitute for you.

Encourage them to get involved in something which doesn't require a keypad or touchscreen and uses more than just their two thumbs to operate. Try martial arts, radio controlled airplanes, dirt bikes, drums, archery, medieval role playing, culinary arts, fashion design, body building, the stock market, whatever. Just give them options and pretty much nothing is off limits. If they do get involved in something, a sport or club, be there every time they compete or perform. Brag openly about their accomplishments, have t-shirts made, put signs in your yard, cover your vehicle with stickers and put kudos in the newspaper. Know about their activity, its rules, schedule, equipment and your kid's role in it. Make sure they know how proud you are of them. You are their biggest fan and it should be obvious to them and everyone else on this rotating rock.

Section 4: Intervention (Sweat the Small Stuff)

The lives of kids are always changing. They're growing up physically and emotionally. At some point the opposite sex goes from being yucky to interesting, very, very interesting. They're trying to figure out who they are and who they want to be. They're indestructible (in their own minds) and scared out of their minds of what lies ahead; all this while trying to be popular with everybody, somebody or anybody. It's tough. These changes are happening to kids all over creation. They happened to us, didn't they? Yeah, what a crazy, mixed up time that was.

Large changes are obvious, so there's no real effort needed to identify what they are, their causes and their probable effects on the kids. It's the small ones that take effort identifying and understanding. Small changes are subtle and can be ongoing for some time before the red light goes off. Small changes, however, may be the stuff you need to pay the closest attention to. Watch for changes in their looks, behavior, hygiene, language, interests, etc. they mean something. When more than one small change takes place at the same time, begin the investigation. It may turn out to be nothing at all but don't underestimate your gut feelings. If you suspect anything, look for proof.

Understand how to check their electronic devices and do it on a random schedule. Actually, go inside the room you provide them and look around. Open drawers, look under the bed, between the mattresses and any place else you'd like for anything you can find. Their room is not off limits to you but yours is to them. Contact the parents of their friends, school officials and so on as soon as you feel small stuff is present. You must find out what's going on even if you're saying to yourself, "I don't want to know." You have to know. You're their parent.

They may be trying to gain acceptance with new people because they no longer feel accepted by their usual crowd. If that's the case, many kids will gravitate to a new crowd with a lower standard of behavior than the old one. This doesn't always happen but it's easier for a kid to lower their standards than to raise them. The new group will accept your kid with open arms and assure them all the bad in their life has been caused by you and everyone else on earth. No one will understand them like the new crowd will and parents are no longer needed to give guidance or support. Hey, if you parents were so great your kid wouldn't be searching for a place to belong, right? Well, I disagree.

The bad in your kid's life is probably very similar to the bad in other kid's lives and the rest of the world probably has had very little to do with it. The bad in your kid's life may be a manifestation of their own ungratefulness, impatience and lack of maturity.

That sounds harsh but it might be true. The new crowd doesn't really want to understand their newest import, they just want more kids to be like them so they feel better about themselves. Parents are not only needed at this point, they're needed more than ever. Looking for, noticing and acting on the small stuff can prevent this scenario from happening. It's much better to deal with small stuff when it's, well, small. It sure beats wrestling with it later when it's grown into the proverbial 800-pound gorilla.

Section 5: If/Then (The Accountability Guarantee)

"If you do that, I will... If you don't do that, I will..." Follow through on whatever the three dots mean or you show weakness. Weaknesses are exploited by kids. Your kids should never be able to exploit you. The actions you tell them you'll take (which are caused by their actions or inaction) must be guaranteed. The kid doesn't need to get ticked off about it since they knew all along exactly what was going to happen. For example; not cleaning their room to your liking means no Internet for the next 650 years, give or take a decade. If they don't clean their room to your liking, their Internet privileges are removed with no discussion or debate. They get the Internet back 650 years or so later, also guaranteed. The length of time I used as an example may be a bit too long in reality. After all, I imagine you want the fruit of your loins to be out of the house and on their own well before the seventy or eighty-year mark.

Now I'll give you some truly realistic examples. I credit English teacher extraordinaire, Jennifer Ertel with this first one. Depending on the age of the child and severity of the parental rule infraction, you can have the child sit in the middle of the room with not talking, TV, music or games. Here's my spin on it. Give them a book and have them read it out loud. Tell them they have to read a certain number of pages before blessed freedom resumes.

Another Ertel idea; if you have siblings who argue, have the main instigator wash the other's clothes, with your supervision, or clean the others room, also with your supervision. I like my car to be looking clean and shiny at all times. I'll bet you do too. If the kiddies need some corrective discipline, they can wash and wax your car or clean the bathrooms or paint stuff or pull all the weeds from the seven-acre vacant lot across the street.

Here's one I used while working as a supervisor in USAF Correctional Custody; if you have decorative rocks around your flower bed or some other yard décor, have your child turn all of them over so the other side gets some sun too. Ok, maybe not such a great idea. Just put their extra energy to good use either by strengthening their reading skills or sprucing up your vehicles or yard. Oh yeah, don't forget the vacant lot.

We've all heard parents in line at the checkout tell their child what kind of trouble they'll be in if they don't put that candy bar down this instant. The child puts it down, then picks up a different one. "Ahaaa" they think to their little selves, a technicality. The parent repeats the future trouble scenario a little louder this time and the child puts down candy bar number two. The child waits until the parent casts their gaze in a new direction, then firmly grasps candy bar number three. Here we go again folks.

I wonder about something. When was the last time the parent followed through with the trouble scenario? Maybe, so long ago their child no longer worries about it. The parent feels they're in control since they're "correcting" their child's behavior verbally over and over again. I think control rests firmly in the hands of the child, along with candy bars number four and five and six and…

By the way, the Internet and all other things in their lives except their basic needs are privileges not rights and can be removed for however long you deem necessary. I guarantee it.

Section 6: Bad, Good and Exceptional (Correct, Recognize and Reward)

Bad behavior in a child can be corrected. Bad behavior in a pre-teen can be corrected but it's harder. Bad behavior in a teen can be corrected but it causes gray hair, less hair, less sleep, the question "Why did we have kids anyway," the statements "Because I'm your father," "Because I said so," "Well, I'm not your friend's parent, so…," "Go to your room," "Uuhhh," "Go ask your mother" and the list goes on and on.

There's been a mountain or two written about teen behavior and how to deal with it. What's right for you may not be right for anyone else so I'm not going to chart any certain course here except to say this; YOU are the parent, period. Your children are dependent on you, not the other way around. Your children may be able to text 3,000 words, codes and symbols per minute and do integrated chemistry and physics (whatever that is) but that doesn't make them any wiser than the other thirteen- to eighteen-year-olds on the planet. They need your wisdom, guidance, correction, love, discipline, humor, protection and understanding. You are that important in their lives. Don't let anyone or anything replace you in these areas. Clearly define your expectations and the boundaries they are required to stay within.

You'll probably have to remind them that the reason you have expectations and boundaries is because you love them so much (this will need to be repeated each time an expectation is not met or a boundary is sprinted past by your kids). Love is your driving force, your motivator and your eternal promise to them. It's your family and you decide what will and will not happen, not your kids.

Good behavior is what we all should be exhibiting. It shouldn't be looked at as a special achievement or something out of the ordinary. Yes, good behavior should be recognized, especially with young children but no one should get a fifty-dollar bill for cleaning their room or taking out the trash. Those things should be done just because they need to be done.

The younger the child the more recognition there should be. This re-enforces that good behavior is worth it. Young children need and want praise and happy dancing and balloons and puppies and cupcakes (who doesn't) and all the stuff that makes them feel special – and they should get it. However, as the child gets older, the recognition should be in line with their age – less whooping it up and more "you did a great job," hugs, thanks and pats on the back. Teens really want recognition that they're doing things right and they want to be treated more like adults. Telling a teen face to face (no text messages please) you notice them maturing and appreciate what you see in them will work wonders.

So, if good, "normal" behavior isn't worth rewarding, what is? I think it's something along the line of exceptional behavior above and beyond the norm. Example: Your kid mows your lawn (hopefully) and you thank them. Cool. Your kid mows a neighbor's yard for 10 bucks (cheap) and you tell them they did a nice thing and didn't over charge. Cooler. Your kid mows another neighbor's yard and refuses to take any payment because the neighbor is elderly and doesn't have much money. You tell them how proud you are of them and that they have shown compassion for someone else which proves they are maturing. Way Cool!

Ok, now comes the reward; maybe cook a meal they choose or take them to their favorite restaurant. You were going to eat anyway and this makes the meal a little more special. Whatever you do, make sure they know you see the adult in them coming out.

Bad behavior must be corrected and never tolerated. Good behavior should be the norm and recognized. Exceptional behavior should be rewarded in some way. The correction, recognition and rewarding of behavior sends the message to the child, teen or young adult that you notice them and care about their development.

Section 7: Obi Wan Kenobi (Why parents and their kids don't see things eye to eye)

In one of those *Star Wars* movies Jedi Master Obi Wan Kenobi told a young Luke Skywalker that many of the things we think are true (or right, or good or bad or whatever) appear that way depending on our point of view. This happens in real life between parents and their kids. Parents and their kids look at life differently, from their own points of view. Parents look at life from their experiences. Their responses to their kids are often, "how much is this going to cost us, you want to go where - with whom - for how long, how many chaperones will there be, is this really for school, what kind of injuries could this cause, will our insurance cover it, if we get it – you have to feed it, you're not old enough" and so on. Kids look at life from almost no experience. Their sales pitches often contain these and other misguided justifications;

1) It will only cost $1,000

2) Can I have it, *pleeeease?*

3) It's just a little fun

4) It's OK, everybody's going

5) It's OK, everybody's doing it

6) I think this one kid's mom might be there

7) It's not like I'm going to get killed or anything

8) Come on, I just wanna go

9) My life will be so over if I don't get these shoes

10) You just don't understand what it's like to be a teenager

11) Just say yes

12) Insurance – whatever

13) I'll feed it, walk it, play with it and everything

and so on.

Parent's points of view are often based on the worst thing that could happen while kids don't think anything bad can ever happen. The worse thing almost never actually happens thankfully, but sometimes bad things do. That's when parents utter the words, "I told you so."

Parents are on the lookout for their kid's safety and their kids are on the lookout for fun. That's an Ok arrangement and the norm in most households. It helps if the parents will explain, in exhaustive detail, their concerns, or why they have just said "no" to something their kid feels is an immediate necessity for their survival on planet earth.

The exhaustive and all-encompassing manner of the explanation isn't designed to bore the kid into an early grave, but reveal details, only the parent may understand. Most kids miss these in their sales pitch. The ones they've missed may be the reason for the dreaded "no" verdict. If the kid goes berserk or falls asleep during the explanation, they're obviously too young or immature to do or have what they've asked for.

Chapter 3: Teen Truths

Section 1: Responsibility (Stupidly Stuff is Important)

You (the teen) want more responsibility or responsibility for the first time in your life. Some of you are a little unsure about the whole responsibility thing because it could result in more work around the house. That means you'll have to give up some of your free time to do it. Some of you may actually not want any or any more responsibility because you're lazy. Being lazy is a natural thing for all of us. Responsible people want to be lazy too but we're too busy being productive and, well, responsible. Taking time off and relaxing is a very good thing but doing nothing but that all the time does not prepare you for the rest of your life.

Ok, back to responsibility and the fact that stupid stuff is important. What stupid stuff and why is it so important? The stupid stuff is the stuff which has an impact on you and maybe your immediate family but really no one else. It's important because it's what your parents are evaluating you on to see if you can handle some real, larger than yourself, responsibility.

I call this type of stuff "stupid" because that's what a majority of the teens I've spoken to call it. You know, stuff like; getting up on your own without being yelled at or having the covers pulled off your bod, actually cleaning your room not just hiding the mess under your bed, cleaning your room without being told, doing the dishes (wash, dry and put away) without being told, taking out the garbage without being told, mowing the yard before it swallows the house without being told, (there's a pattern emerging – can you guess what it is –

without being told) doing your school homework without being told, feeding the dog before it gets so hungry it tries to chew someone's leg off, asking permission for things you're supposed to ask permission for, not talking back or mouthing off, coming home on time, answering text messages from your parents even if you don't like what they say and so on and so forth.

Those actions, if done properly, may just convince your parents that you're growing up a smidge and deserve a higher level of good 'ol responsibility. You might be thinking you're ready right now and maybe you are, but, if you're not getting more responsibility (and trust – they go together pretty well) then maybe your actions don't scream it loud enough to be heard.

It's possible you've been neglecting the "stupid" stuff in hopes it won't be noticed by those withholding gold plated responsibility from you. Look, if your parents don't see you being responsible for the stuff I've just mentioned, there's almost no way they'll give you anything substantial. You won't get big time responsibility if you can't even handle dragging your carcass out of bed on your own or if you whine for the millionth time about doing your own chores.

Totally made up example time. You can lift fifty pounds but want to lift eighty. You hang out at a gym regularly but refuse to work out to get stronger. You insist to every one you can lift the eighty pounds but the gym owners won't let you try. You get ticked off at the gym owners but they still don't let you try. It's obvious the gym owners know nothing about lifting weights and are only holding you back, right?

What's really weird is that the gym owners can not only lift the eighty pounds you want to lift but can lift a whole lot more. In fact, they carry at least eighty pounds around with them all day as if it was nothing. You don't care. You want to try to lift eighty pounds but have only lifted fifty a few times in the past; most of the time you lift about twenty-five pounds or so and sometimes have to be reminded by the gym owners to do that. No responsible (there's that word again) gym owners are going to let you try to lift eighty pounds when your max right now is fifty and your usual weight is no more than twenty-five. I hate doing math problems but even I can figure this one out. The more you act on your current responsibilities, the stronger your responsibility muscles will get.

If you aren't responsible for what you have now you shouldn't be given any more responsibility. It's not your parents fault, it's yours. You can fix it though, by simply taking control of your own current responsibilities. In other words, do what you're supposed to do without being told or whining or telling your parents every time you do something. Just do it and move on. Once your parents notice this change in your behavior they might just offer you some heavy responsibility for a change. Actually, you'll have earned the chance to prove yourself.

Totally true example time. While in Air Force basic training I noticed something I thought was a little funny. It wasn't my instructors. No, they weren't funny at all. In fact, I don't believe they had the slightest idea of what a sense of humor was or how it could be used in a social gathering. They were loud, foul mouthed and in a perpetual state of being ticked off. They did tell jokes sometimes, though. That was awkward. The jokes weren't funny at all. The instructors would tell them and then stare at us waiting for our response. The airmen in my basic training flight would laugh and laugh, just to be on the safe side.

We were all there to become airmen in the most powerful Air Force in the world. Some of us had legal contracts which secured our job training choices. There could have been future aircraft avionic mechanics (for the world's most advanced fighter aircraft), special operations combat search and rescue or security forces nuclear missile security training ahead for some in my flight. The instructors didn't care. Some tested extremely high to get their job choices. The instructors didn't care. Others, like me, went in with no contract and selected our job choice in the second week of training. The instructors didn't care. We were a fairly smart group of young go getters. The instructors didn't care. They didn't care because we hadn't proven ourselves yet.

What struck me funny was that we were given almost zero responsibility for anything but our own selves. In fact, every single part of our lives was dictated to us. Things like, when we'd get up (it was called Zero Dark Thirty, aka; 4:30am), when we would turn the lights out before going to bed (9:00pm – we'd get to sleep around midnight after we'd gotten everything ready for the next day using only our flashlights), which urinals, toilets and sinks in the latrine (bathroom) we could use, exactly how we were to wear every piece of our uniforms (including underwear), when we could speak, what we could and had better not say when we did, where we could and could not walk, what we could and could not eat and drink and so on.

I distinctly remember the six-inch ruler. We had to fold our T-shirts and underwear in perfect six-inch squares or face the wrath of the humorless instructors. How stupid, right? Wrong.

There was no way the United States Air Force was going to give us anything more than our own t-shirts and underwear to be responsible for until we proved ourselves worthy. No weapons, missile guidance systems, aircraft parts or cyber linguistic secured international communication do-dads for us.

No way, it was t-shirts, tooth brushes and metal bunks. That's all we could handle at first.

Let's face it, if an aircraft mechanic puts the wrong wire in the wrong place it's a recipe for disaster once the jet punches through the sound barrier or some other cool maneuver like that. We had to learn that the 6-inch square t-shirt was as important to us then as the proper wire placement would be to the fully trained aircraft mechanic later. We had to prove our ability to handle responsibility, no matter how odd or stupid or unimportant it seemed to us at the time. We had to use the tools they provided to us without whining about it or not using them because we disagreed with the whole idea.

Note: There is no whining or disagreeing in basic training. Well, you can, but if you do, trouble will find you. Our trouble was named Technical Sergeant Upton. He stood about 6' 5" tall (without the Smokey the Bear Hat!) and wore an immaculate uniform. He was a Blue Rope which meant his hat had a blue cord around it – which meant he was in the top 10% of all Basic Training Instructors. Technical Sergeant Upton always found us.

That six-inch ruler went from being stupid to one of the most valuable pieces of equipment we were allowed to work with. It helped us produce perfect six-inch square undies; at that time, a very important achievement.

We began receiving more and more responsibility for ourselves, our exercises, movements, classes and so on as time went by. Those who failed to meet the strict standards were "washed back" a week to do it again. There was no second wash back – that was called being discharged. We either had what it took to move ahead or we were sent packing.

Here's the difference. We wanted to excel. We wanted more responsibility. We wanted to be worthy of the title Airman and maintain the standards of those who were serving and those who had served. We were motivated and no one had to tell us to do what we knew we had to do. It was that simple for us. It's that simple for you as well. You should be motivated by a desire to excel as a teen ager and no one should have to tell you what your responsibilities are or that you haven't met them.

Section 2: The 14th Year (Childhood Is Over! It's about time. Aren't you glad?)

I've said it before and I'll say it again; childhood ends when you leave the middle/junior high school. You're about fourteen so you've had a good run of being childish and irresponsible. It's ok not to have had a lot of responsibility. Some kids that age are given too much and miss some or most of their childhood. Either way, childhood is a thing of the past once you step away from the middle school/junior high. It's the proper time in your life to look ahead and not just to the next five minutes but months and years ahead. You can stay a kid forever if you're filthy rich and can pay people to take care of you as if you're a helpless baby, but why would you? Instead, make some plans for what you want out of life and start moving in that direction. It's your time.

Actually, you should be glad to be moving on. You've had fourteen continuous, uninterrupted (I hope) years of being a baby, child, kid, pre-teen and now, new teen. The middle teen years are upon you and it's time to jump in all the way. You shouldn't feel like your life is over and the world is against you. Don't get your feelings all wound in a knot because higher expectations of your behavior are now in place. Show your parents, friends, teachers, coaches, strangers, aliens, whoever, you're ready, able and willing to move on. Again, it's your time.

Section 3: Turning from Childhood (Accepting Reality – Proving Yourself Worthy)

I just said a few words about childhood being over once the middle school/junior high school is ancient history. The transition from child to full teen often requires "turning your back" on the thoughts, language and activities of childhood. You get to replace them with better versions. If you hold on to childhood it'll show in what you think about, say and do. You'll blend child and teen together into some mutant nobody will understand. You don't want that. Neither does anyone else.

Section 4: Disrespect (Keep it to yourself)

Showing respect in any form is good for you and the person you've shown it to. Calling a man "Sir" or a woman "Ma'am" won't dent your coolness factor. Saying please is a good way to get what you want. Saying thank you is a good way to get what you want the next time you ask. Being respectful can soften the mood of those you speak to. It can control their attitudes in a way. These words make people feel good hearing them and make you look good saying them. If there's a negative part to this, I don't see it. If you do, you're immature.

You don't even have to feel respect for another person to show it. You can hate them and be respectful. It can be your little secret if you feel you need that type of thing. By the way, showing respect never gets you in trouble, not showing it just might.

If you don't respect the person, you probably should respect what they do. Usually, persons who warrant (are expected to receive) respect have something you want or are in authority over you like parents, teachers, police or coaches. Showing them respect is expected and noticed when it's absent.

You want respect too and you want it from the very same people who should receive yours. I doubt you'll get much respect from them if they're wondering where yours went. You might be asking yourself why you should show them respect before they'll show it to you. The easy answer is, because they were here first. Since they were here first, they have responsibility for and maybe authority over you. They may not want either but they have it. They carry that burden, you don't. Show them respect by words and actions and you'll get some back.

Section 5: The Big Lie (Adolescence)

Yeah, this one's going to make a few people mad I'll bet. I know there are all kinds of descriptive terms I'm not about to use here, like pre-teen. I don't really mind them but for the sake of not naming every conceivable age descriptive title out there I'll stick with four.

In my opinion (that's all this book is, really) you are either a baby, child, young adult (teen) or adult. Notice, adolescent is nowhere to be found. Childhood ends when you leave the middle/junior high school. Being a young adult is a time to show by your words and actions you're ready to handle more personal responsibility. You shouldn't even want to be a child any more. You had 14 straight years of it. Aren't you tired of it yet? You should be. Your goal is to be more adult than young as years pass. Holding on to childhood when you're no longer a child is ridiculous. Adolescence is an excuse that holds young adults back from their development. It does nothing to help. Don't fight adulthood, embrace it.

Section 6: "Boys will be Boys" (Lawsuits will be Lawsuits)

That "boys will be boys" thing is something I heard when I was, well, a boy. It used to mean, for the most part, harmless fun. Oh, maybe a prank or two to add spice to our lives, but nothing immoral or illegal. To imply that a boy, by his very nature; that is, being a boy, should be allowed to get away with something because he is, in fact, a boy – is – discriminatory toward girls. We could say, "girls will be girls" and allow them to be as irresponsible as the boys. Yeah, that's the ticket. Then all the boys and girls could run around with their "get out of trouble free" cards and not be held to proper standards of behavior. No Sir, I don't like it. I don't want to take away from harmless fun or even silly pranks. I'm a giver and a taker. I've been pranked and I've pranked right back.

While living in Egypt, courtesy of the Air Force, the site I was on (Wadi Qena) was visited by a Major General; that's two stars. To make him feel at home (in his expandable living quarters) I assisted in, short sheeting his bed. Furthermore, I was selected to – push the General into our makeshift pool – while he was still in uniform – it was a nice uniform – full of all the awards and rank insignia which clearly identified him as someone – you don't push into pools. When I found out I had been volunteered for this assignment I wondered what the Federal Penitentiary at Leavenworth, Kansas was like. I figured I'd find out soon enough.

This is how it went down. The General was standing near the pool edge giving a speech. I (Pawn #1), was on his right side; his star-studded shoulders shining in the desert sun. Another low-ranking airman (Pawn #2), was on his left side. We were given the "green light" via a wink, or nod or something clever like that from someone clever like that. We were about to initiate "Operation Kiss Your Rank Goodbye." We paused for one last moment before sealing our fate, then, the General grabbed Pawn #2 and threw him in the pool. The two-star boss reached for me next but I jumped back, so, he grabbed the nearest airman (a Master Sergeant) and threw him in. Then, he jumped in on his own and ordered his aide, a full bird Colonel, to do the same, which of course, the Colonel did. Good times.

Let the kids have their fun, just don't lower or remove the guidelines they and every other kid should follow. That way the fun they have doesn't end up getting out of control and turning into something they'll regret (or have to apologize for, or pay for, or get stitches for, or cause someone else to get stitches for, or talk to a judge for, etc). Control. It's everywhere isn't it?

Section 7: The 18-Year-Old (It's only a number.)

I hear 18-year-olds saying they're 18 years old all the time. I know full well what turning 18 years old means and what it doesn't mean. I wonder if the 18-year-olds who want everyone to know they're 18 years old truly think there's some kind of transformation that's going to take place changing their dull and powerless 17th year to an all-encompassing, euphoric, nirvana like, power tripping 18th year? It seems so from where I'm sitting. Many of the newly minted 18-year-olds I've met have tried their best to exercise all-encompassing euphoric nirvana like power on others around them simply because they've blown out 18 candles recently.

Ok, ok, so you're 18; big deal. Instead of quoting your number so much, try acting like it. Better yet, act older. The fact you brought up you're 18 (or soon will be, or will be in a year, or two or ten) proves you don't get what it represents. It does not represent a magical transformation taking place in the world around you. It doesn't mean you can do whatever you want. It means you are responsible for whatever you do. If you really were so mature you'd know this. You won't be instantly smarter or better looking and you certainly won't be any wiser.

The rest of us don't go around spouting off our number (age) in an attempt to prove our point or get our way or get out of trouble or for any other reason in which our age is irrelevant. We just go through life trying to do our best. We try to make good impressions on those around us without actually letting them know our age.

Yes, turning 18 is actually pretty great. You get more freedom and responsibilities and society looks at you as an adult in almost every way. Listen to me here. You're not going to always get your way because your 18th year has finally shown up. You still have a lot to learn from those of us who've passed 18 two and three times. We want to help you navigate your 18th year and beyond. My number is 52 (as of this writing) so I got ya' beat in the "what's your number" department. I and most other "older than 18-year-olds" will explain what we know to any 18-year-old who cares to listen. We have wisdom and don't mind a bit passing it on. If you don't ask, you'll never receive. If you never receive, you're on your own. So, you're 18 now, congrats. Try not to mess it up.

Section 8: True Friends (Your Best Interest Investment)

Many of your friends - are not. A true friend always has your best interest in mind. A true friend will understand the differences between the two of you. A true friend will cheer you when you win and console you when you lose. A true friend will sit next to you, not saying a word, when there are no words to say. A true friend will confirm you are right even if that means they are wrong. A true friend will tell you when you are wrong and keep telling you if necessary. A true friend will do what they can to protect you, even from yourself. A true friend will stay when others leave. A true friend will argue with you at the top of their lungs then leave with a hand shake. A true friend will "beat the crap out of you" if need be to keep you from hurting yourself. A true friend will worry, stress, freak out and cry over you. A true friend will let you go if you refuse their help and are determined to head in a bad direction. They're not turning their back on you. You're no longer who they were friends with. A true friend will wait for you to return with open arms, a smile and a friendship ready to pick up where you left off, then happy dance and scream at the top of their lungs, because you're back!

Section 9: Your Comfort Zone and the Dog Leash (Who really has control and why?)

The first demonstration I ever used to help teens understand the importance of having control over their actions, emotions and self-esteem was with a hypothetical dog collar and leash.

If a kid is willing to behave in any way outside their comfort zone because of another kid, they need to "buy" a dog collar and leash. Once they've purchased these items (chosen to properly accessorize their current wardrobe, of course, duh) they place the collar around their neck, hook the leach to the collar and hand the business end or handle of the leash to the kid whose opinion of them is more important than their own. See, this clarifies their relationship; the leash holder is the master and that kid is their pet (or slave). Again, this is hypothetical.

We all give up control over parts of our lives sometimes (sport practice and game schedules, work schedules, dress codes, curfews, money/taxes, etc.) I'm not talking about that. I'm talking about giving up control of what you do and how you feel about it. If you want to wear the latest fashions, great, do that. If you want to change your diet or start exercising, great, do that too. If you want to do something you've never done before and it won't hurt you or anyone else, great, get started. If, however, the reason you're doing any of those things is for the approval of another person, be careful. If, you don't really want to do those things but will, for the approval of another person, stop. You've just given up control of your actions to them. Your emotions will follow and your self-esteem will take a nose dive.

At least some of your actions, like what you wear, who you hang out with and the kinds of things you'll do are now in the hands of the other person because they're holding the leash. Your emotions are inside you but they can be manipulated so easily. You won't even realize it's happening. Then one day, someone, a family member let's say, will ask you what's wrong or say you look depressed. They'll say it's been going on for a while but thought it was just a phase you were going through. It's not a phase. It's that stupid leash pulling that stupid collar which is securely attached around your neck. The more it's pulled, the more you're controlled. The more you're controlled, the more your emotions become irrelevant. The more irrelevant your emotions become, the more of your self-esteem gets flushed down the toilet.

Example time has come. Let's start with a big one, sex. Girls: if you don't want to have sex (or anything close to it) don't. No one should have control over your body but you. Get it? In fact, no one should so much as touch you unless you approve. That goes for having pictures of you (almost) wearing something.

Speaking of wearing something; you shouldn't be forced to wear anything you're not comfortable with. No means exactly that, no, negative, ain't gonna happen.

Guys; some girls will drag you by that collar straight to fatherhood. They want a kid (that's a son or daughter to mature people) and will do anything and everything to get one, or two. Sexual desire is one of the strongest (maybe the strongest) powers of the leash which happens to be connected to the collar around your neck, which happens to be connected to your body.

What about friends? If your friends aren't the leash holder's friends, then they aren't your friends either, anymore. Before you strapped the collar around your neck and surrendered your wants and desires to another person - you had your very own friends - but not anymore. You've had to stop hanging around them, talking, texting, tweeting, or in any way, communicating with them. The leash holder doesn't like them. They were stupid anyway, the leash holder says so. The only friend you need is the leash holder. The leash holder said that too. Aren't leash holders smart? I hope my sarcasm has been loud enough.

You don't (I hope) stay out to all hours, talk back, sass, smart off or cuss out your parents, shoplift, trespass, smoke dope and a host of other socially unacceptable, immoral, illegal, stupid and dangerous crap now; but, you might if you're pulled hard enough. I mean, why not? The leash holder wants you to. Do it, go ahead. What's the worst that could happen? I'm sure the leash holder will come to your rescue, or pay your bail or visit you in the hospital or be at your funeral. Your funeral is the only time they will voluntarily give you back the leash but you won't need it then.

Lets' say you've already "bought" a collar and leash to match. You've given it to someone else or maybe a group.

They've had control over you to whatever degree, and you want that control back. You'd like to be your own person again and make your own decisions. You haven't felt right about things in your life for a while and it's time to feel right again. Here's how you do it. Go to the leash holder or holders (if there's more than one, you'll be feeling worse because you've been jerked around by more than one jerk) and tell (don't ask) them to give your leash back. Take it. Now, take the collar off and throw both the leash and collar away, stand back and take a deep breath of freedom. It'll feel good.

When I said "go" and "tell" concerning the leash holder, it was meant metaphorically. That is; decide you'll no longer "go" the way they dictate and you'll "tell" yourself what's right and wrong from now on. Getting control back from a leash holder is difficult sometimes. You can still be friends with them if you want, but that is a decision you should make on your own. It's a mental thing. If you need help, help is available from the right people. Ask your parents, teachers, pastor; whoever you feel you can trust. They won't ask for or accept a leash. They want your actions to be safe and enjoyable, your emotions to be healthy and happy and your self-esteem to be strong and as high as possible.

The freedom to make our own decisions about what we like or don't like separates us from creatures who need that level of control. We don't need to be controlled like that. We need freedom, the freedom to decide right from wrong and the wisdom to seek help from good people when we're unsure. This is a win, win situation for all of us. We win if we have the freedom to choose for ourselves and if we seek help from the right people when answers aren't clear. My advice to you is, win as often as you can and keep the collar and leash out of it.

Section 10: Your Friends the Guinea Pigs (They'll show you what not to do.)

If a friend tells you about something that has happened in their relationship which you respond with "you should dump him/her for that," it tells you what you should do in a similar situation.

We usually don't act as quickly in our own relationships as we advise others to do in theirs. If it's good enough for them it's good enough for you.

Section 11: Verbal Bullies (Predictable - How do they know all this stuff? – It's all about me!)

Let me start by saying, I fully understand how serious bullying is. What I'm going to talk about are ways to coat yourself with self-confidence, use humor to deflect the bullies taunting and maybe distance yourself from the manure they spread.

Let's say you're walking down the hallway at school just minding your own business, when suddenly, you hear something nasty about you or an accusation about you or some other ridiculousness fly through the air and land in your ear. You have just been verbally bullied. Congratulations! Congratulations about what, you're probably thinking. I'll tell you a little bit later.

Now let's say, after passing through the verbal bully's best attempt at ruining your day, you realize you forgot something and turn around. You head back from whence you came and again hear the sounds of stupidity from the knucklehead. I'll bet if you strolled past the little darling one more time they'd say something mean and nasty, again.

There seems to be a pattern forming here. You walk past – they say something stupid and hateful – you walk past again – just like clockwork, they say something moronic and mean – a third time by and (you guessed it folks) a third time some form of insult laden proof their gene pool is pretty shallow bounces off your cranium.

Joking aside, look at the situation here. You walk by and they say something bully-ish. It happens every time. You could walk back and forth in front of them all day and they'd try to come up with some witty trash to talk. That's predicta-bull crap right there. Predictable bullies do the same thing to the same people in the same circumstances. If you have a predictable bully and you know they'll say something ugly to you when you're near – why let it bother you? You know it's going to happen and happen it does, right on schedule.

Verbal bullies like to accuse people of things, as well as, make fun of them. They'll say you did this or that, with him or her or them, while drinking this, snorting that, smoking the other thing and are now infected, infested or pregnant. Wow. How do they know all this stuff? I mean, they'd have to follow you around chronicling every move you make in order to be this savvy as to your life and its style. I think they're just making stuff up because without your life to talk about (which they make up), no one would listen to them. It's all lies but that's all they have to give.

You don't have to feel crushed because some teenager makes up a lie about you and is willing to repeat it whenever you occupy the same hallway they do. These pitiful things may not be able to form an actual independent thought on their own. What they say is designed to be hurtful (and deep inside it does sometimes) but you must maintain control of the situation by not giving them the satisfaction of showing it. You're a better person than they are (yes, I said it). You aren't weak and you certainly don't want to lower yourself to their standard. You are strong and you have something on your side they don't. Fans.

Your mind is now singing the soft refrain of "The author has really lost it this time." Not really. This mental coat of confidence is something I began using as a junior in high school. But first, my bullying story.

My brother was a junior in high school when I arrived as a freshman. He stood 6' 7" tall, was a star basketball player with legs the size of redwoods. Some kids in school didn't like him and wanted to bully him. They, however, did not because Sam was 6'7" tall with legs the size of redwoods. They waited for his little brother to arrive so they could bully him instead. Enter, me.

I was shorter, smaller and had asthma until 7th grade. Just paint a target on my back and get it over with will ya'? Some kids didn't like me and wanted to bully me. Well, they all (his bullies and mine) just had the best of times bullying and picking on your truly. It let up as my freshman year went on but never fully stopped. My sophomore year went a little smoother but still had its rough patches. At the end of my sophomore year I realized something. Try as I might, I could not bring myself to actually care what the bullies had to say about me, my friends, international finance or what they had for breakfast. My best efforts to give a rat's rear end about their feeble attempts at insults bounced right off me. Back when I cared about their insults, they stuck to me. Now that I didn't care, they just went "boiiing." That's a good feeling.

I was upset about one thing though. I was upset (just a little) with myself for having cared so long. I mean, I was a teen and so were they. We all lived in the same area and everybody knew everybody. Everybody knew they were verbal bullies and nobody believed what they had to say. No one believed them because, hey, it's them. I decided to look at them in a totally reversed way. They stopped being my bullies and became, my fan club.

Here's how it worked for me. I realized that every single time they had said something to me (no matter how ugly it was) they were talking about, me. They – were talking – about me. What they had said wasn't a good thing but I didn't care. They were saying it about me, which means their previous conversation had ceased and had been replaced with words about, me. Me, Me, Me. This happened simply because I walked by. Hey, this is kinda cool. They could have been talking about really important stuff in their lives like their confusion over what deodorant is used for and how to spell their own names. Then, I'd appear, and everything stopped. Their conversation is now directed toward, me. I could halt their ramblings about other topics any time I wanted by simply exposing them to my presence.

What they said was made up, hurtful and hateful crap but I no longer cared. Even if what they said had been true, I really don't think I would have cared because it would have come from them. They're opinion of me meant nothing. Remember, bullies of this type are predictable and make up all the crap they say. No one (worth concerning yourself about) believes them.

At times I found myself laughing out loud a little at what my verbal bullies would say. I couldn't help it. I knew something rotten would be said when I strolled by, but, it went from being hurtful and intimidating at first to weird and irritating and finally, stupid and irrelevant. That would make them mad so sometimes they'd say things they thought would be worse. I'd try hard not to, but sometimes, I'd laugh harder. They had gone from being my own personal verbal bullies to my own person, fan club. A mean spirited and creepy fan club for sure, but a fan club none the less. I had mentally put them into a new category, one that couldn't hurt me anymore. Fans don't hurt the people they adore, they admire them and talk about them. I doubt my former verbal bullies ever admired me but they sure did talk about me a lot. Goody for them. It was just talk; predictable, made up, fantasy world, impossible for them to know, ridiculous, no longer hurtful talk. That's all it was and I absolutely did not care in the least.

If you currently have your very own verbal bully or bullies, now is the time to begin changing your mind about them. Take control of your emotions and transform your bullies into your fans. Understand this; you know when they'll talk about you, what types of things they'll say and the reaction from you they expect. They will talk. They will say pretty much the same things. You can't control that part of it. Your reaction, however, you can and you must control. If you control your reactions to them, you win.

Hopefully, with your reactions firmly within your control, your verbal bullies will begin to fade away. If they no longer can get the reaction from you they want, you'll no longer be any fun for them. Since they'll be getting a reaction from you they don't understand, you may become a mystery they can't solve. You'll be off their list of victims. Oh well, it will leave them more time to investigate the complexities of spray verse stick.

Section 12: Cyber Bullies (More chicken than verbal bullies.)

If they're not bully enough to say it to my face, there's absolutely no hope I'll ever care what they type. Maybe they could make a party of it. Yeah! They could invite all their friends, type some dumb made up crap about me then do arts and crafts, like, painting yellow stripes down each other's backs (a sign of being a coward). Yeah, yeah, yeah; so you think you don't like me. Uh, huh. Ok. Well, good talk.

Section 13: Physical Bullies (The line has been crossed.)

I've often wondered why physical bullies always seem to get it wrong. To be truly recognized as a well accomplished bully in the bullying world, you'd think they'd (to coin a phrase) pick on someone their own size. Better yet, to show their prowess at the bullying arts, they'd pick on someone larger than themselves. Does this happen? Of course, it doesn't. The physical bully is too scared for that. How can we be impressed with a bully who picks on someone shorter, lighter, younger and far less aggressive than they are? Anyone can do that.

I think the finest example of a physical bully would be one who messes with someone at least 50 pounds heavier than they are and several inches taller. If they ever tried bullying someone older, taller and heavier than themselves – Presto, no more bullies.

A physical bully must be identified and their actions reported to the proper authorities immediately. Once identified, every bully action, no matter how small, must be reported immediately. Not a single bully action they perform should ever be allowed to happen without notification. If nothing is ever said about their intimidation tactics, physical contact and assaults on others, why should they stop? Did you get that? Why should they stop if no one is going to say anything? Well, they shouldn't. Actually, they should but you know they won't. What's stopping them from doing worse things? Since nothing is being done about them preying on others, they up the ante and become even more violent. They certainly don't fear being identified or held legally accountable for their actions if everyone stays hushed.

Physical bullies almost never begin with the worse thing they can do to their victim. They work up to it. They pick a victim, then, do their stuff. Nothing is said about it so they do a little more. Silent, so here comes something worse. It can lead to ritualistic abuse that will leave the victim hurt physically and emotionally for the rest of their lives.

Since the physical bully has control of the situation, they decide when (if) it stops. They aren't physically or emotionally messed up, only the victim. The physical bully just replaces one victim for another. They usually have several at a time. Are you kidding me? Somebody say something! Scream it if you have to. In fact, screaming at the top of your lungs is a nice reaction when some low life tries the slightest physical bullying. They may think you're crazy, but it makes one fact crystal clear; you are not an easy victim. Never be an easy victim. Never be an easy victim. Never be an easy victim.

Here's a specific true story about me being physically bullied. I'm a freshman in high school and not the biggest guy around. It's August of 1979. Two, yes two, larger than they outta be freshmen join our class from parts unknown. Of every boy in our class, they picked me to bully. What a pile of crap this is. I had one in my gym class and the other in my math class. Oh yeah, the one in my math class sat right behind me. What a pile of crap this is. Gym class was bad enough. It was showering after class that was a nightmare. Few of us showered, really. More deodorant and a comb through our hair then out the steamy, body odor filled locker room we went. I had to navigate this humid stinkfest while avoiding this monster who desperately wanted to flush my head down the toilet. That little maneuver was/is called a "swirly." I hated going in the locker room. He knew it. I was terribly intimidated, scared out of my mind and willing to do just about anything to avoid even going to gym class. I dreaded it all day. It made my stomach hurt, I lost my appetite and even thought about it when I tried to sleep. That was the none-physical part from this bullying tag team.

The physical part came during math class. As I said, the other bully sat behind me. Simply put, he poked, slapped, hit, stabbed, flipped and in all other ways, hurt me whenever he could. It was painful to me but never noticed by the teacher. She had her back turned, writing some mathematical concept on the board which, to this very day, I have no concept of.

I tried moving forward, sitting side ways (which only exposed my ribs – dumb idea) and anything else I could but nothing worked. I was so afraid of both of them I resorted to carrying a "weapon" in the halls. I made it out of a pencil. I didn't sharpen it. I removed the eraser and stuck a thick sewing needle through it, then super glued the eraser back in place.

After walking around a couple days with it (resulting in several small puncture wounds in my hands and arms) I decided I had to do something smart instead.

LISTEN UP TROOPS: The sewing needle idea was bad in every way, so is any idea that even resembles it. I told you that to show how desperate a kid can feel and what kinds of ideas that desperation can produce. DO NOT do this yourself. I mean it!

Once I had come to my senses, I deduced nothing would work on either bully if I tried to meet force with force. I had to say something to someone or they'd never stop bullying me or any of the other victims they had, of which they had several.

I had had enough and was now mad. So, I began. I told my folks. Mom called the principal. I told my math teacher. She asked me to point him out. What? You want me to point at him where he can see me? Let's get it on! I pointed right between his eyeballs and made sure he and everybody else in the class saw me. I did the same in gym class. The two idiots were called to the Principal's office, then, I was. The principal told me I should have come to him sooner. Yeah, yeah, yeah; I was petrified, alright. I thought, I'm telling you now so start doing principal type things to them.

He said something to me the two muscle-bound morons would regret. He told me to tell him every time they did or even tried to do something to me. I can do that, I thought. So, I did. I decided to turn to "The Nark Side" and take back control. Narcs, snitches and tattle tails are some of my favorite kinds of people.

The "narc side" went something like this. Either of them hit me – I narced. Either of them shoved me – I narced. Either of them threaten me – I narced. Either of them stand in my way not letting me pass – I narced. Either of them do that head jerk thing which looks like they're going to head butt me – I narced. Either of them so much as look at me in a way I found threatening and I narced. Each time I narced the principal called them to his office. He got tired of it real quick. He took it out on them, not me. I was the victim, they were the predators. Their other victims started narcing as well. It was a glorious narcfest. Let's see, knowledge is power, right? You bet it is. Every time these two boneheads did anything within the emotional or physical bullying realm, that knowledge was passed on to the principal. Hence began the personal avoidance policy. It's not what you're thinking I'll bet. Let me explain.

At one point, I turned a corner and spotted one of the bullies. He was walking toward me. He turned around and went down another hallway instead of getting close to me. He realized nothing was going to go unnoticed or unreported - nothing. He had developed a personal avoidance policy of me. He would avoid me, not the other way around. I was in control now I was never going to give it back.

Both bullies left our school before the end of the first quarter. I don't know what happened to the one in my gym class. I saw the math class offender in handcuffs being escorted out of the building by two rather large deputies. I was in the right place at right time to observe this little slice of justice. I hadn't reported anything about either of them for a while so I don't know what caused him to be given such pretty bracelets via the two heroes in uniform. I admit I felt a sigh of relief. Alright, alright; I was thrilled to see him go.

If you're being bullied, in any way – report it - <u>now</u>.

Section 14: The Mechanic and the Dentist (Check your advice givers number.)

I have a mechanic I take my car to for repairs and a dentist I like to take my teeth to for all kinds of interesting procedures. The mechanic and the dentist are both experts in their fields. When I need advice about what might be wrong with my car I ask my dentist. When my teeth hurt, off to the mechanic I go. This works just as well as going to the mechanic for my car and the dentist for my teeth, because, my dentist drives a car and my mechanic has teeth. I figure they're perfectly capable of giving advice about the other's profession, right?

That makes as much sense as one teenager asking another teenager for advice about something neither of them has ever experienced. The topics range from relationship woes, checking and saving accounts, how to build their credit, their future plans and how best to get there successfully, taxes, should they really meet in private with the person they've been messaging to "hang out" because that person really understands them and could never be a sexual predator, could they, how to dress and speak during a job interview, vehicle maintenance, personal safety, coupon collection and usage and the list goes on and on.

Sure, reality TV, movies and sitcoms are out there to provide truly realistic scenarios about life (sarcasm). However, I think a real person, old enough to have lived life as it happens (without a script), is a better choice.

The teenager only advice scenario can go something like this; Teen #1: Hey, what should I do about this? Teen #2: I don't know, try this. Teen #1: Will it hurt? Teen #2: I don't know, just do it. Teen #1: Is that legal? Teen #2: I don't know, just do it. Teen #1: I don't know about this. Teen #2: I am, just do it.

If you need advice about something outside the realm of teenagedom, ask someone outside the realm of teenagedom, like parents, teachers, counselors, coaches, principals, pastors, mentors and anyone else who's already faced this situation. What they say could save you from a lot of bad mojo. Their words might even set you up for some serious success.

As of this writing, my number (age) is 52, really old right? Wrong! If you're a teen reading this, your number is between 13 and 19. My number is higher, much higher. Therefore, I am wiser than you. I didn't say smarter, I said wiser. I've seen the work kids have in high school these days and its way past what

I did back in the early 80s. I'm not talking about book smarts here, I'm talking about wisdom.

Basically, wisdom is the knowledge of what is true or right, coupled with good judgment and actions; in other words, the understanding of what should or should not be done. Isn't that what you're looking for, understanding? Only people who have experienced something have a true understanding of it. Instead of turning to your friends (smart as they may be) for advice about something they can only guess at, ask someone with a number that's about double your own. The bigger their number, the more wisdom they may have – the more wisdom they have, the better advice they can give – the better advice they give, the more you understand. Isn't that the reason you asked the question in the first place?

Section 15: The High Bar (Have quality in your life)

If you're a teenager, the chances of you being with your current boy or girl friend in 5, 10, 15 years and beyond are almost zero, zilch, nada. You're supposed to be looking for "the one" which may take some time, like years not days.

Each relationship must be taken slowly so you can identify "deal breakers" and any other annoying or bad habit they have which will drive you to the funny farm. You'll also identify your own oddities. It all helps you define the qualities you must have in a partner and the qualities which bring the funny farm closer.

The bar (standard) you have must never be lowered as it relates to the person you may spend the rest of your life with, every second of every minute of every day, day in and day out forever and ever. You deserve the highest quality person in your life and only you'll know what that means.

Section 16: The Age Difference (We're all the same at the same time.)

I was young once. I remember when cell phones were the size of bricks, there were no i-anythings or e-anythings and the Internet was nowhere to be found. I've been around a long time. So why do teens think I don't understand what it's like to be one? Ridiculous. I know perfectly well what it's like. I've already been there, survived the ordeal and moved on.

Teens are going through physical, emotional and social changes all at once. It's rough. I went through the same thing. It was rough then too. They want more freedom, so did I. They're anxious, scared, confused and excited about the future, so was I. They're breaking up and making up, so did I. See, we're all the same, when we're at the same age. When emotions are in use, the decade they're being used in doesn't really matter. Teens are teens are teens.

I think it would be nice if the teens of today would be willing to openly communicate with the teens of yesterday about stuff. The "persons formerly known as teens" could give some advice or just listen. Sometimes that's best. When the teens of today realize the teens of yesterday can actually understand what they're saying – real conversation can take place. I'm talking about real, helpful, healing, bonding conversations. New teens, middle teens, old teens – we're all the same. Let's talk.

Section 17: Privacy (The best way to protect your privacy.)

Help me out here. Why do people explain, in exhaustive detail, the last argument they had with their significant other? They chronicle every nasty thing said (by the other, not their own nasty nouns and verbs) and the emotional stress it has caused them. This is done from the privacy of their own homes but sent out to the remaining members of the human race to scrutinize.

I guess their aim is to get others (who are not part of the relationship) on their side, thus putting them in the relationship in a sort of digital Peeping Tom kind of way. More and more people now know they had an argument, what it was about, how they felt about it (like that's difficult to figure) and that they'd like them to join in solidarity against the aforementioned significant other. Pathetic.

Actually, they've turned their significant other into their insignificant other. If they were a significant part of the relationship, the argument would have been kept between the two of them and hopefully they'd be able to work things out. Instead, they hold the argument in "public" for all to read. Some people openly argue in front of total strangers in public places. That's awkward and usually caused by a dual spontaneous outburst of frustration. At least it's not a typed, punctuated, thought out, play by play of an unfortunate argument between people who actually (maybe) care for each other.

Now for the help I need. I don't get it. Can you help me understand? It's bad enough people will post their private arguments. What's worse is, the posting person will get their feelings all bent out of shape when someone makes a comment they don't like. Then, another argument starts for the entire world to see.

I've heard that people who make negative comments are called "haters"; maybe so. Maybe, just maybe, they're simply having a laugh, at the poster's expense. The argument laden essay may be the most fun the hater has had all day. They don't care if there's an argument and that two (or more) people are hurting. They'd like it to continue to provide them with something to smile about. Pathetic, the sequel.

Privacy is important. So important in fact, it should be kept secret. I figure most of the drama in people's lives is caused by them. If they kept their mouths shut and their phalanges off the keyboard, touchscreen, or whatever they use – their world would be a better place. So would ours. If you don't want others to know something, don't splatter it all over the World Wide Web. If you want a new batch of haters though – send your deepest, innermost thoughts and feelings into the great www.world. Your current haters and the haters who don't even know they hate you yet will be waiting. They'll jump on the band wagon I'll bet. Then, you'll have something else to deal with. Classy, just classy.

Section 18: Privacy, The Sequel (Someone is looking for you.)

This is going to be short and not so sweet. You do not know anything true about anyone on the other side of your computer or phone. When you message someone (you don't already know) about the things in your life which tick you off, you're talking to a stranger. Who are they, really? You have absolutely zero idea.

They may be looking for weaknesses you'll expose to them. They may be gathering information about you and you don't even realize it. They may be saying exactly what you want to hear at exactly the right time to lower your guard and convince you to meet with them in person – without telling your parents – because this computer stranger has been where you are or is going through the exact same thing you are right now (what a coincidence).

Personal information about your emotions, stresses and wants may be just the thing they need to set you up for a meeting with them and their true self, not the one they sent you via their computer or phone. When you meet them, they may not be the age or even gender you thought they were. Their idea of "hanging out" may be criminally different than yours.

Internet predators target through deception (lies). They'll profile you as a potential victim then ease their way into your mind and emotions. When they think you're at your most vulnerable, say, mad enough at your parents to leave for the night or run away altogether, they strike with a helpful way out. They'll offer to pick you up and take you where you want to go or let you stay with them for a while. If you go with them – you're going with a stranger. It doesn't matter if they look just like the picture they sent you and act exactly like you hoped they would.

Once you get into their vehicle you are at their mercy (if they have any). Once inside their vehicle you may meet their friends (accomplices). Now you're outnumbered by strangers in a small enclosed environment being taken, somewhere. Not a good scenario at all.

Your privacy as it pertains to emotions, stress and relationships should be looked at like financial privacy. People try to keep their credit card numbers, social security numbers, bank account numbers and such very private. Why? Financial predators are constantly trying to steal them. Exposing too much personal information to a (wait a minute – back up) exposing any personal information to a stranger can put you in a very dangerous situation. You start giving control away which will bring your vulnerabilities out. Once out, the predator has something to chew on.

Protect yourself by talking directly to the people who can help you with a problem, not just to anyone with a computer. Sure, you can gripe about stuff, we all do, but not to the point you open yourself up to the influences of the unseen, unknown stranger trying so very hard to "help."

Section 19: Reactions (Yours determines theirs.)

Hey teens, ever wondered why your parents act the way they do when you ask them for something? Out of the blue, they go freakazoid all over the place and all you asked was if you could stay out an extra hour with your friends. If they didn't want you to, they could just say no. Instead, they turn into stark raving grouchasauruses. I'll tell you why. They may not be acting but reacting to, you.

What I mean is, their reaction to your request may be a direct result of the last reaction you gave them. They may have uttered words like "take" and "out" and "the trash." Maybe horror reached your ears when you heard "homework" spew from their vile mouths. Your reaction may have been something far less than cooperative. You might have had a blockage of your common-sense gland and actually said "no." By the way, saying you'll do it later and not doing it is just "no" in disguise.

Whining, that's a good one. Whining about doing what your parents say is a good way to get a freaky reaction from them later. I know you get frustrated at all the rules, chores and stuff your parents put on you but your reaction to them can set up a good or a bad reaction from then later. It's only natural.

Look, if you don't cooperate with them it gives them every right to go grouchasaurus on you when you ask for a favor. Fact: You cop an attitude when your parents ask you to do something. Fact: They look at you as ungrateful for what you have. Fact: You don't understand this and later ask them for a favor. Fact: This causes freaky grouchasaurusness from your parents. Their minds go berserk trying to figure out why on earth you'd ask them for a favor after not doing what they had asked. Fact: You still don't understand this and gripe about it. Fact: It doesn't help.

Cooperation is a two-way street. If you're asked to do something and you react in a negative way like, saying "no," whining, talking under your breath, slamming doors, saying "this is so dumb," asking "why do I have to," stomping your feet saying "whatever" (which is "no" in another disguise) and so on, expect a less than overjoyed reaction from your parents when you ask them for a favor. Again, it's only natural.

If you get the freaky reaction from good old mom and dad, have the common courtesy to stand there and take it, then, acknowledge your earlier mistake, apologize for it and politely ask again. They may still say no but they may just switch gears and say yes because you did the mature thing, you know, admitting your mistake, apologizing and asking again in a polite manner. You may be saying to yourself, "This dude's crazy." I've been called worse. Crazy or not, I know you'll have a better chance of getting what you want by being mature and nice to the parental ones than being a whining, uncooperative pain in the gluteus maximus.

Section 20: It Takes Time (You'll be here anyway)

"Good things come to those who wait." That's a nice sentiment, but a load of crap if waiting ain't your thing. But wait, look at it this way, you're not waiting, you're getting closer. What am I trying to say? The time it will take won't be spent waiting, it'll be spent doing. I'll give you an example.

Let's say you want to learn to play the harmonica to a proficiency level which won't cause dogs to howl, small children to cry or the cops to be called. You go to your local harmonica training center and ask the resident harmonica guru how long this type of endeavor will take. The guru responds, eight months with daily practice. I've never played harmonica so don't flip out if I'm way off on my time frame. You think that's way too long and leave the harmonica training center in dismay.

Eight months later you're still alive and you still can't play the harmonica. You're still alive and you still can't play the harmonica. Say it with me; you're still alive – and – you still can't play the harmonica.

If you plan on still being alive at the end of the time needed to accomplish something, you might as well get started and accomplish it since, you guessed it, you're going to be alive anyway. You could, of course, explain to others how you were going to start learning the harmonica eight months ago but didn't because it would have taken eight months.

During that time, you'll probably be on *Facebook* a lot, have taken about 1.5 million selfies, commented on several billion posts from people you know and don't know and a host of other really, really, really important stuff. Yeah, that's much better than trying something new, isn't it? Maybe so, but I think differently - big surprise huh?

I think all the really cool, awesome, radical, outrageous, technical, complicated and daredevil type stuff out there takes time to learn and perfect. I mean, earning your black belt in Karate doesn't happen over the week end. The journey to your black belt is part of the fun. As you improve, the time spent is justified. There will be many special moments along the way. Once you've reached your goal you may look back and ask yourself, "where did the time go?" Time flies when, well, you know.

Section 21: Been There, Didn't Do That (Surviving the lie)

Oh boy, here we go. I hope you're sitting down. Prepare to be shocked, awed, propelled into a world of disbelief and the realization that the impossible, is truly possible.

I have never had a drink (alcohol) or a smoke, dip or chew (tobacco) or a smoke, hit, injection, snort, etc. (drugs) in my life. I went through school with kids both similar and very different from myself. I left home and joined the military. I've lived overseas. I've worked multiple jobs. Like I said, I've been there and there and over there, but never did that or that or that. I've been around all kinds of people in all kinds of circumstances with all the usual, and a few unusual, temptations.

I decided long ago I wouldn't do certain things for my own spiritual, personal, moral and or course, legal reasons. So, all this bovine fertilizer about "everybody does it" or "everybody tries it at least once" is a lie. I'll make my own decisions thank you very much. It's one way of maintaining control in this somewhat out of control world we live in. You can make your own decisions too and you should do just that.

Don't let what others say make you feel obligated or pressured to do something you simply don't want to do. It's ridiculous to believe the "everybody" argument. Stand your ground while keeping a firm grip on the all-important control aspect of the decision-making process. Then, make your decisions based on what you, not others want. You'll have to live with your decisions. You may have to explain them at some point down the road. You might even have to face the consequences that result from those decisions. That's ok. It sure beats living with, explaining and facing consequences for a decision someone else conned you in to.

Section 22: My Life is Crap – Send (Well, hmmm, not everyone has a cell phone)

It seems a lot of people these days feel a sense of entitlement. Your first thought is that I'm talking about teenagers, isn't it? Well, they are the major guilty party here but not the only party here. Let's "pick on" teens anyway, Ok? Ok.

When I worked at the high school, I was surrounded by teenagers for eight hours per day, 180 days per school year. Almost all of these little darlings had cell phones. Almost all of them had a vast variety of clothes they alternated wearing. They also had money in their pockets, accessories to their ever-changing wardrobes, vehicles (nicer than mine), braces to straighten their teeth and a host of other additives to their basic needs. They emphasized their lousy lot in life by griping to every other kid in the same comfy condition they were in. They griped, therefore they were. They griped with such dexterity and grace. It was a ballet of bull biscuits performed – on their smart phones.

Some mild examples, if you please. These well-off teens would issue complaints about the following topics of agony.

This list is by no means complete but a mere portion of a much larger list of perceived injustices.

1) Not having the newest and best smart phone to issue complaints on.

2) Not being given (given actually meant the parent had to buy it) the newest and best replacement thing to replace the last thing their parents had bought which the teen had left, oh, somewhere, they think.

3) Not being able to go and/or do what they wanted, when they wanted, with whomever they wanted, for as long as they wanted; gimme, gimme, gimme – let me, let me, let me – crap, crap, crap – send, send, send.

Most kid's lives are not crap. A kid who is neglected has crap in their life. A kid who doesn't have enough food has crap in their life. A kid who is abused has crap in their life. A kid who lives their life in real fear of something has crap in their life. Most kids have a good life no matter what they say or what they say it on.

An overly complaining teen should visit a homeless shelter or soup kitchen. They could spend some time with special needs kids. Maybe time in these environments will jerk the overly complaining teen into reality. Maybe they'll appreciate what they have and who gives it to them. Maybe they'll get a monster dose of grow up and cool the complaint-fest they've been on. Wouldn't it be nice, just once, to read, "Life is good?" Yeah, send that.

Section 23: D-O for the B-O (Do you smell something?)

Use deodorant for your body odor. The end.

Section 24: Words from the Toilet (I am not kidding)

Let me explain, it should make sense in a few minutes. This little tidbit of info can save you and your parents a heap of trouble. The great thing about it is it can be used on just about every subject you and your parents disagree on.

If you and those who made you or are taking care of you don't see eye to eye on a subject, or many subjects, or any subjects, this is for you. If whenever that certain subject comes up it turns into an argument, then shuts down at about the 20 second mark, you'll have more to say that never has a chance to get out. That's twenty seconds or so of mutually exchanging different points of view before, BAM, bring on the screaming, door slamming, accusations and the inevitable, "Because I said so," "No, and that's final," 'I don't want to hear it" and so on, hits the fan.

Believe it or not, this isn't productive. It hasn't worked in the past, it's not working now and all indicators say it won't work in the near or distant future. Try something else. How about a letter? Yes, a letter. A letter which contains every last word on the subject you've never been able to say. A letter which holds the reader hostage and informs them of all the stuff you've been trying to get out. Thank you, thank you, yes, it is a great idea.

Start the letter by saying something unexpected like, I Love You. Yeah, that'll throw 'em off. Seriously, start by telling them you love them and are writing this letter so there won't be an argument. Make it clear you want to communicate with them in such a fashion they'll get to hear what you've never been able to say before, you know, without all that pesky yelling getting in the way.

Ok, now for the content. Say everything you ever wanted to say on the subject. For the ending, say you love them again and sign it. You thought this was going to be complicated and painful, didn't you? What to do now? You've taken care of the words part like the title says, but there's still the toilet to contend with.

Don't flush the letter. I don't think it's really necessary to write that, but why take any chances? Tape the letter to your parent's toilet. They should find it pretty easily. If they don't after a couple days, you have another problem on your hands and should probably write another letter.

The letter should be taped in place just before you leave for a while and they'll be home. If you're home, they'll just read the first sentence or two, then find you waving the letter back and forth and ask, "What's this all about?" Next, comes the argument.

Your parents need to be alone with the letter for this to have a chance of working. When you get home, they'll probably come up to you waving the letter back and forth and ask, "What's this all about?" That's to be expected. What happens next will hopefully be a conversation. At a minimum, they'll have read every word you have to say on the subject. It might help. In fact, I've been told it has. It's worth a try isn't it?

Well, that outta do it.

Section 25: Being taken seriously (Walk their walk and talk their talk)

If you want to be taken seriously when you speak, and I suppose we all do, you should speak in a way the hearer feels comfortable with. They shouldn't have to work at understanding your message nor should they hear the exaggerations you may use with your friends to make your message seem more interesting.

If the person you're talking to, and really want to be taken seriously by, is not a teenager you'll need to lob non-teenager type nouns and verbs at them to help them understand what you'd normally say in your own unique brand of slang, made up words, and exaggerations. Also, be brief. The more you try to "sell" what you're saying, the less likely they are to "buy" it.

A decade is a pretty long time. If you haven't reached your second one yet and you're talking to someone in their third or fourth, it's best to speak to them the way they would speak to each other. If not, you run the risk of not being taken seriously. You want to have control of your message. You don't want your message controlled by the wrong words.

Don't forget, the excessive use of the word "like" is bad. Like, in saying like you have something, like, really important to say and, like, it's the most important thing you've ever said like in your whole life…like. After the second "like" no one is listening anymore.

What about non-verbal communications? Yes, they are important to being taken seriously. My dad always says it's not what you say it's how you say it. He's right. Your tone of voice, voice inflections, volume and changes in pitch add to the words you're saying. What they add better match the meaning of your words or you will send mixed signals. Control of the message you're sending will be damaged if that happens and you'll end up having to explain your message again. Never put yourself in a position to explain your message more than once.

Here's one that might make you mad. What about your look? Does your look help or hurt you when you're trying to be taken seriously by others? Yes, you can look any way you want. Yes, no one should judge or discriminate against you because of how you look and yes, you should be taken as seriously as anyone else no matter what you wear, how you wear it, what you pierce, what you pierce it with and what your tattoos look like and where you have them. However, you will be judged and possibly discriminated against for those very reasons and the words you use in your message by some people. Heck, you may be discriminated against or not even be allowed to speak if the hearer doesn't feel comfortable with an aspect of your outward appearance. Don't get ticked off about it, it's normal.

If people don't like what they see when they look at a person they probably won't be very willing to listen to that person speak. If they are willing, they may have formed opinions about them which that person's message will be filtered through. I'm not saying it's right, I'm saying it happens. Get used to that one; things not being right but existing anyway. That's called life on earth.

So how do we navigate this? You might not like this one either. It requires change, temporary change. Change you can change out of once the need for the change is over.

Let's say you're going for a job interview to be a secretary. BTW: secretary means office assistant to most folks. Office assistants do secretary work so I call them secretaries. Secretary takes less time to say than office assistant or administrative assistant or office administrative clerical oversight engineer specialist associate.

Back on track now. The company you're interviewing for has a modest and professional dress code. You arrive for your all-important interview in an 80s hair band concert t-shirt torn jeans and flip flops. Just turn around and flip flop away.

You could show up in attire resembling what you'll be wearing if you get the job (good choice) but your hair is died blue. Just turn around and walk away.

How about clothes that match the company's image, hair the color which grows out of your head but a gleaming chromed plated nail is sticking through your ear with an accompanying chain running to your nose ring? About Face – Forward March.

The bleeding skull tattoo should be covered until you get the job and find out how the bosses feel about such a decoration. Maybe they have one too but the interviewer may not. They're the person you need to be changing for at least for the length of time it takes to get through your interview.

The change(s) you make for this interview may need to become part of your life during the hours you work for that company. You change back to your usual self when not at work. This too is normal. It's part of getting what you want in an environment unlike what's normal for you. The same is true in reverse. If the company is casual and you show up in a suit or dress the interviewer may think you're not a good fit for that company's environment.

This is a pretty easy one if you think about it. Be who you need to be, where you need to be it to achieve your goal. It may not be a comfortable situation as it relates to what you wear or the language you use but if you want to "fit in" enough to secure and maintain the job you'll do it. You'll do it and laugh once you realize you've learned to "play the game"; the game of adapting to your surroundings for your own benefit where you'll be taken seriously, as you should be.

Section 26: Invisible Good Advice (The forest and the trees)

Maybe you've heard the phrase "you can't see the forest for the trees" at some point in your life. It explains if you're so focused on one idea or concept (a tree), you could miss seeing the other ideas and concepts around you (the forest). Good advice is like this. We can get it but not see it because we refuse to shift our focus toward it.

Warning: I'm about to talk about political type stuff. My disclaimer this time is that I am not now, nor have I ever been, a politician. I am a voter. The following is not a political statement or manifesto of any kind. I am not forwarding any political agenda. I am merely using the whole tree and forest analogy with references to persons who have been or are now politicians. No need to protest in the streets or block by driveway or call me names ending with "-phobe."

During the 2017 presidential election, it seems Hillary Clinton had a favorite tree. She spent her time on the campaign trail staring at it. Her tree was, her firm belief that what she was doing on that trail would lead her to The White House. She was wrong. No, I'm not bashing her or her political party or anyone else in her political party or our political system or politics in general, so calm down if you thought she would win.

Mrs. Clinton campaigned the way she wanted to and received advice during the campaign while she did it. The way I see it, the advice came at her in three categories; good, bad and neutral. In reverse it goes like this; neutral advice is what she received which wouldn't hurt or help her. The bad advice was no doubt given with no ill intent toward her campaign but it would have (and maybe did) hurt her if she took it. The good advice was given to her from many sources. These sources were supposed to be close to her but really weren't. They were in the same forest as she was but not near enough to her tree. These sources moved about the forest looking at what was going on, questioning the forest inhabitants and developing strategies for her to consider. She didn't consider them because she didn't take the time to focus on them, only her tree.

Now we come to the strange part. Even her husband, former President Bill Clinton, gave her advice. Good advice as it turns out, if she had taken it. He had spent two successful presidential campaigns in the same forest with the same trees and won both. His advice came from the perspective of his successes. Part of his advice was for her to campaign in states she hadn't up to that point; states that wanted change in a big way. Those states were like trees she refused to look at. Her opponent, presidential candidate Donald Trump was indeed campaigning in those states talking about the big changes he wanted to make.

When she debated Mr. Trump she didn't take the good advice she was given to specifically say what she would do to make changes for the better. Mr. Trump did. The advice that her campaign strategy wasn't working well enough wasn't acknowledged. The fact that she would draw crowds of hundreds when Mr. Trump was drawing crowds of thousands was met with no alteration to her stare. She was being given good advice, which basically said, she needed to campaign a little more the way Mr. Trump was. The result was more staring with all that good advice going to waste.

Mrs. Clinton lost the 2017 presidential election. Mr. Trump won. Mrs. Clinton, those around her and many more across this country and the world were shocked at the election results. So were many who voted for (now) President Donald Trump.

Both candidates Clinton and Trump had something in common during the campaign. They both had good advice given to them. Mrs. Clinton decided to focus on her way and her way only (her tree). President Trump didn't choose a tree to focus on, he chose the forest. He decided to look at it as a whole, move through it and talk to its inhabitants about what mattered to them. If there is a moral to this it could be; good advice is invisible if we refuse to look at it.

What about you? Are you so focused on something or someone you refuse to listen to the advice of others? I hope not. If you are, don't you want to know what their advice is? Aren't you even a little curious about what others may see or know which you may not? It's not going to hurt you if you listen. My daughter Sandra told me years ago that she'll always listen to the advice Cathy and I will give her. She then stated she may not always follow it, however. That's cool. I want her to listen which she does. What happens next is her decision. My point; she will always listen. You should too.

Here's a way to help you decide if advice is good or not. This isn't fool proof. Of course, what in life is? When you receive advice, decide the age of the advice giver (20s, 30s, 40s) and so on. Now, find two other people in the same age group. Tell each of them YOU have had an idea and tell them the advice you've been given. Since it's now an idea in your head you can claim it. Make sure you don't say who your advice giver was or who else you'll be talking to. If both people say your idea is good = good advice. If both people say your idea is bad = bad advice. If one says good and the other says bad = you're on your own! Seriously, you probably should ask more people to get a general idea of what to do.

All I'm saying is; listen whenever people you trust have advise for you. Listen to them then make a decision. Whatever you do, don't become so focused you ignore others around you. It could cost you a relationship, a successful business, a promotion or even a job opportunity you've convinced yourself you can't lose.

Section 27: How to solve pretty much any problem (Time Travel)

Have you ever found yourself in a problem situation and wondered how you'd gotten yourself into it in the first place? I think we all have. If the answer doesn't pop into your brain right away, you may need to take a little trip back in time to find it - the answer that is. How far back you'll need to go is often determined by how deep you are in doo doo at that time. The deeper the doo doo, the farther back you go.

This problem-solving technique, while not absolutely perfect in every single way, is worth trying; or, you could just stand there wading in the doo doo hoping a miracle happens soon. Just for the sake of argument (and to keep you reading) let me explain the time travel idea.

Once you've firmly established there is a problem about this or that, slam on your brakes and stop. Go no further – going further could make it worse. What I mean by go no further is, don't make any more decisions or take any actions concerning the problem, just stop.

Now, take a laser focused look at the situation you're in. Be very, very specific. Try to identify exactly what the problem is and how you're involved. You'll also want to identify what the problem is doing to you. You'll need this knowledge as you travel backwards.

Once you have the knowledge you need about the problem, turn around and look back in time. Look back to the beginning of that day, the previous day, the previous day before that and so on. Be very, very specific. You're looking for the problem's starting point. This will be the event, statement, decision or misunderstanding which kick started the problem you now find yourself within.

The pattern may look something like this; everything is "normal" then something out of the ordinary happens and your version of normal is thrown out of balance. You try to keep your normal afloat but don't actually do anything substantial to correct what's happened. The problem builds. Since your normal is out of whack, the events, statements and decisions you make from then on are out of whack as well. So, the problem worsens.

Once you've identified what has thrown your normal into a tail spin you can hopefully do something about it (if it's not too late). But what do you do? Turn around again. Start making substantial corrections to the things that went wrong from the moment your version of normal went by, by. Correction may require fixing a misunderstanding, giving apologies, accepting blame for your actions or forgiving others for theirs. Do what must be done to bring normalcy, as you define it, back to your life. It may not be easy to do. It also may take a while before your corrections catch up to the present day. The way I see it, if you want to fix the problem you'll be willing to put in the effort; unless you decide to take up doo doo wading as your newest hobby.

Section 28: Hating what you're doing (It's Ok)

I've always been told that hate is a strong emotion; well, duh. I've also always been told a person should never hate. I hate when I hear that. Ok, Ok, I get it and it's pretty much true. How many of you readers out there think there's going to be a "however" coming soon? You would be correct.

However, hating what you're doing may be unavoidable, depending on what you're doing, of course. Wouldn't it be just peachy if we all loved what we had to do all the time? Yes, it would. Is that ever going to happen? No, it isn't. We're left with the distinct possibility we may not like some of the things we'll have to do in our lives. Worst case scenario; we may, in a very real sense, actually hate some of the things we'll have to do in our lives.

What should you do when, not if, this worst-case scenario grabs you and won't let you escape? In the simplest terms; do it and hate it at the same time.

Do: Whatever is required of you and do it to the best of your ability.

Hate: Whatever you're doing - which is required of you - which you're doing to the best of your ability.

You liking what you're doing is in no way necessary for you to do it to the best of your ability. Actually, you liking it isn't necessary either. It helps, but it isn't necessary. You could feel no emotions at all about what you're doing and still do it to the best of your ability. Are you catching on yet?

If something is required of you, like; homework, housework, job work, getting up on time or being somewhere on time; that's all that's required – no emotions are necessary. Zip, zero, nada. You aren't evaluated or judged or inspected on how you feel about what you're doing. You're evaluated, judged and inspected by whether or not you did it and how well it was done. If you've done well (even though your emotions were being stomped on at the time) you'll have every justification to feel the happy emotion. If you've done poorly or not at all (because your emotions were being stomped on at the time) you'll have every justification to fell the crappy emotion.

Rarely, if ever, will someone ask; "What emotions were you feeling while you were doing that?" All too often you'll simply be asked; "Did you get that done?" This is sometimes followed by; "Did you do it right?" Ok, that's where your "I'm Ticked Off" emotion could make an appearance and I understand that. It's entirely possible you'll be asked that last question because you've not done whatever "it" is correctly in the past. It's also possible the person asking you is simply a jerk. Check out what I have to say about bosses for more on that.

Bottom Line: Always do your best no matter how you feel about what it is you're doing. Don't even mention how you feel, especially to whomever has told you to do the thing. All they want is for it to get done. Sure, they'd like you to be happy enough in your work but if you're not, it really doesn't matter. Doing matters. Doing to the best of your ability matters. Consistently doing to the best of your ability matters. Having your emotions in perfect balance with the universe – zip, zero, nada.

Chapter 4: Relationships

Section 1: The Good, the Bad and the Ugly (Let's take a ride)

I've talked to quite a few people in my life who described their relationship with a significant other as being in the bad or ugly category. It seems people in the good relationship category don't talk about theirs much. They just live in the relationship until the topic of relationships pops up and those around them start complaining. If they speak of the good in their relationship to those in bad or ugly ones, they're often not believed. No one can be that happy and contented in a relationship, can they? That's not what relationships are for. They're for making those within the relationship miserable, right? Actually, that's not supposed to be true but is true far too often.

Relationships produce an interesting phenomenon I like to call "The Emotional Roller Coaster." Have you ever ridden a roller coaster? I've only ridden one in my life and didn't like the experience. It pushed, pulled, twisted and bounced me all around the tiny, tushy unfriendly seat, then shot out like a rocket only to slam to a sudden stop to the many shrieks of the weirdoes who actually liked it. A real roller coaster is bad enough in my most humble opinion, so an emotional roller coaster has got to be a nightmare gone bad.

Speaking of bad; I've got bad news for you I'm afraid. If you're in a bad or ugly relationship, you're riding the emotional roller coaster right now. If a relationship you're in now goes south, you'll be riding it next. There's no way to get around it.

Once you step out of a relationship, you step in line to ride. Sure, some relationships end amicably without too much mess but even those will put you in the tushy unfriendly seat for at least one trip around the emotions. Since you can't avoid the coaster – ride it with gusto. What I mean is, don't suppress your feelings. Let them out (in a healthy way of course).

Holding the inevitable flood of emotions inside you means they're not being dealt with. You're going to have to deal with them eventually so stop trying to push them down or stomp them into oblivion. It won't work. What will work is, take your reserved seat on the coaster (your emotions about the relationship, the break up and your uncertainty for the future will have made the reservation for you) throw your hands up and let the emotional twisting and turning begin.

I'm crazy, right? Maybe, but I have a definite reason for what I've just said. That reason (as if it's gonna come as a surprise to you) is control. Bludgeoning your emotions into some dark crevice of your psyche isn't controlling them. They'll be back and will probably show up when you least expect them at the most inopportune time possible. Emotions are like that. I think controlling your emotions when they're frayed means dealing directly with them as much as possible. I did not say you'd have total control over them, I said as much as possible. A little control is better than none at all. No emotional control, whether that means a person has "lost it" and acting in a bazar manner or has shoved their emotions into the bowels of Hades, still results in no emotional control. Just like self-improvement or learning a new skill, control of emotions after a break up takes the turtle method, slow and steady.

The emotional roller coaster will take you to feelings of confusion, sadness, anger, regret then back to confusion and who knows what else. Since they're your feelings you can trust them. You'll be able to deal with them in an honest manner and slowly get results; clarity instead of confusion, happiness with yourself instead of sadness, happiness with yourself instead of anger and satisfaction with yourself instead of regret. See how the focus is on you and not the relationship or the other person who was once in it? You're on the roller coaster, with your emotions, so the focus must be on you. That's control.

Where does this control come from? Most of it can come from within you in the form of your own self-reflection and honesty. If you were wrong in some way during the relationship, you'll have to admit it to yourself and use that knowledge to not make the same mistake in the future. If you were wronged, you'll have to understand something very important. That is, you were the victim of, not the cause of the harm.

Counseling is another avenue to gain control. Professionals can provide excellent services to help you. Life coaches can also be used to help you identify and understand what your wants and goals are as they pertain to control.

As time passes and you find yourself in "a better place," you'll have developed a lot of control over your emotions and be near the end of the ride. In fact, most if not all of your emotions will be flying solo again without the need of special attention. That's good. You may even enjoy the home stretch where you have your self-confidence back and look forward once again to the near and distant future.

The emotional roller coaster is a ride no one wants to go on. It can hurt and be a little scary. Most want to get off before it's completed its course. However, the ride is essential. The ride helps you re-gain control over the emotions you may want to suppress, as long as, you don't have to think about them or the person you were once with. Since you know darn well you will think about them and him or her, you're better off riding through the inevitable twists and turns to reach real lasting control over your emotions. Dealing with, not suppressing your emotions will result in you getting control over them before they get control over you.

Section 2: Jerkectomy (Boy Friends/Girl Friends Part I)

A jerk is a boyfriend or girlfriend who lies to you (ever), tries to control you (friends, phone, family ties), insults you (ever), ignores you (ever), treats you like a slave (do this, do that) or anything else shy of being your friend.

An "ectomy" is a surgical procedure which removes something bad. Have you figured it out yet? If they stop acting like a friend, cut them out. They're not "the one." Perform a "jerkectomy." You'll feel better.

Section 3: The Alphabet Test (Boy Friends/Girl Friends Part II)

We all start out with an "A" boy or girlfriend. After some time, their grade can change.

Once the honeymoon period is over they become a "B," "C," or "D"; still not too bad. Their little quirks that used to be cute can start to irritate a little and push them into the "E" through "I" range.

The more unpleasant habits you discover the farther down the alphabet they go. Habits like; forgetting to pick you up when needed, ignoring you, or worse, poking fun at you in front of their friends, vulgar jokes told with you near, the whining about or refusal to participate in things you like to do, the dismissive attitude toward having a meaningful conversation with you (but they'll talk for hours with their friends about worthless topics), acting like they don't know how to help clean up after themselves, displaying the attitude that you exist to serve them, and the list goes on and on; "J, K, L, M, N," oh my. Just a while ago you had a "B." You'd love to have an "H" right about now. A couple hundred arguments later and you've got yourself a "P" through "T." What in the name of lasagna is this? At that point you'd give just about anything for a lousy "M." What the heck happened?

Ok, ok, what to do now? You decide to work on this in a civilized manner. They blame you for what's wrong (maybe some of that is true). You admit your faults and honestly apologize. They don't. Can you say "U" through "W" – yes you can. You finally realize what has to happen next. They need to be put in their rightful place in the alphabet and in your life.

They need to be your "X." They'll ask you "Y" which tells you they've paid no attention to what's been going on since they were a "G." If they ever ask you to take them back, you better say, "Only in your dreamZ."

Section 4: Justification (They'll prove you right.)

If a former boy or girl friend you've just ended a relationship with bad mouths you, has their new boy or girlfriend bad mouth you or has their friends bad mouth you; it proves you were right to make the decision to be free and single again. It doesn't matter why you made your decision. You made it and that's final.

That kind of back stabbing behavior from your former boy or girl friend shows who they really are. They'll make up lies about how they really dumped you and all the terrible things you did to them. Even though it stinks to have someone you once cared about do this, it should satisfy you that your decision was correct and you can move on happy in the knowledge you got out when you did. You were right to say adios and they just proved it. Congratulations!

Section 5: How much more can you take? (It's a matter of time)

This one really works. If the relationship you're in seems unbearable and you think you can't go on any longer – you probably will – go on longer. You've known unhappiness for a long time now, and in a way, you're used to it.

A long time can be determined by percentage. If you're relationship has lasted ten years and you've been miserable since year six, then forty percent of your relationship has been miserable for you. If you've only been together for two years but you've been miserable for one, you've had fifty percent misery time. Some people have a smaller misery percentage, some have more. Many times, a person's misery percentage, although high, still isn't enough to motivate them to make a move.

By the time you reach this point in a relationship, plenty of conversations and screaming matches have probably taken place. Ultimatums have been issued and broken time and time again, so have promises. Deal breakers have come and gone and the relationship (which in no way resembles what it started out as) has deteriorated into, misery. If that sounds like you and your situation, I have something for you to think about.

If what makes you miserable in the relationship cannot be changed and you've honestly tried everything you know to make things better (especially if the other person should have made the effort, or some effort or a little effort but won't) ask yourself this series of questions. Can you remain in this relationship for five more years? That's half a decade. If the answer is no, what about four or three? If it's still unthinkable, try two more years. That's seven hundred and thirty days of what makes you miserable with no hope in sight. Too much; what about one year or maybe eight months? The people my wife and I have talked to so far have all settled on less than six months.

When you've come to your decision, you've just admitted to yourself the relationship is in fact over. You've also determined the maximum amount of time you can remain. You're starting to take control over this unfortunate situation and have set a goal. The goal is, leaving the relationship (in the best way possible) within the amount of time you've decided.

Making this decision should strengthen your resolve and prevent you from blowing a gasket when you've reached your absolute emotional end. The decision you've made is designed to prevent that and give you a time frame and direction to go in. It's a good thing.

There's work to be done. You need to start the leaving process in advance of the actual deadline you've chosen. It's a little different for each person but going from in to out of a relationship usually involves some paperwork, changes to addresses and credit cards and the sorting of things. Compromise is always good but don't let go of anything you really want. It's all part of the control process.

I'll close this one out with the following; being miserable should never be the norm or even an option in a relationship. If you've tried everything you can think of to make things work and none of it has, it's time to put time on your side. It's time to determine how much time you have left in the miserable relationship, then take that time to take back control.

Section 6: Bad People and Your Life (DO NOT let them in.)

Some people are just bad. Yeah, yeah, yeah, I know, there are no bad people, just bad things people do. Bull Crap! There are bad people; they're the people who do bad things. That's exactly why they aren't called good people. Bad people not only do bad things but they want to do them and have little to no regard for others. They'll chew us up and spit us out if we let them get close enough. They'll do everything possible to find a way in and destroy us from the inside out.

In a relationship, the bad in people is hard to see, especially if you're looking through eyes blurred by love or lust. That love or lust can, and will, be used against you in as many ways as possible by a bad person. These people are relationship predators. You'll go along with it, because you don't see it. Others will see it and tell you what they see. You'll hear them but you won't be listening. You'll be too busy having your backbone removed. Eventually, your every move will be controlled and you'll no longer be you, you'll be theirs.

They may start by using their bodies to entice you and then control you. Remember that control thing I keep talking about? They'll trap you in a relationship through children, threats, debt, secrets, and so on.

Let's go in reverse order.

Secrets: They'll find out everything they can about you. The less you want people to know about a subject, the more they want to know about it. If at any point you don't cave in to their will, the last people on earth you want knowing about it will be the first they'll tell. Yeah, that's love alright. It may not even be anything from your past. They'll put you in situations (or poses) you don't feel comfortable with. It's said, a picture is worth a thousand words, or a thousand regrets.

Debt: Your money is their money – their money is their money – your debt is your debt – their debt is your debt.

Threats: Pick a topic you can be threatened with and "Presto" the threat will be laid out in gruesome detail. They don't love you, they love controlling you.

Children: Perhaps the most powerful tool one can use to control another is through children. The threat, "You'll never see your kids again" is paralyzing to a truly loving and caring parent. At that point it may be time to fight like mad for sole custody. Not knowing where your children are or who they're with is absolutely and positively unacceptable.

They do not fear the spotlight and are always the victim. They may hurt themselves (and your kids) in order to hurt you. They can always leave you because they don't love you, they love themselves.

Look up the definitions and characteristics of a *narcissist*, a *sociopath* and a *psychopath*. You may find the person whose behavior you find hurtful, hateful, dangerous and intolerable has been partially, if not completely described. I'm not diagnosing anything. I'm saying look it up. Seriously, look it up and prepare to be shocked, then circle the wagons and protect yourself and your family.

Section 7: Our Story (Time – Connections – Love)

The Time: Cathy and I spent the first 40 or so years of our lives not knowing each other. Until the year 2002, Cathy lived in Canada where she's originally from. We met in May of 2007 after her son Luke, who was in one of my study hall classes, asked the question, "Hey Mr. Hulse, what's a Color Guard?" So, you see; Luke is the reason this whole adventure got started. I have to thank him for that. Luke is a fine young man. He's married and the father of four children. He's a member of the Army National Guard and trains with an Infantry unit. He's also a reserve Police Officer.

The Connections: Luke tried out for the Color Guard and made it, thus, Cathy became a Color Guard parent. She was the best. She never once missed a game or performance. She would

This is our son, Luke; he and I have an interesting relationship don't you think?

Officer Surette at your service.

sometimes have to work a double shift before a performance, then, volunteer to transport kids and equipment. After the performance she'd go home and get a couple hours sleep and return to work. That's true devotion to your kid.

A year before Luke tried out, Sandra, our "God-given daughter" joined. She's the other connection. Cathy and my relationship was nothing more than coach and parent while Luke and Sandra were in school. Luke brought us close by joining the Color Guard. Sandra kept us close after Luke and she had graduated. Sandra joined the United States Air Force after graduation and would alternate calling or writing us letters. We'd then call each other to spread whatever news she had. The connection between Cathy and I was growing stronger.

The Love: Sandra (the little schemer) made sure Cathy and I kept in contact with each other and would drop little hints to us. You know, hints like, "have you ever thought about dating Cathy" or "you and coach (as she called me then) should get together." Subtlety is not one of Sandra's strongest characteristics.

We both assured her things like, it wasn't the right time and she/he would never be interested in the other and blah, blah, blah. Well, the attraction was there and we both were realizing it. My realization came when I admitted to myself I was making up reasons to call Cathy without being contacted by Sandra first. I'd call to ask if Sandra had contacted her, then, when she'd say she hadn't, I'd starts a conversation about pretty much anything just to talk to her.

When I knew she was coming over (to show me the newest letter from Sandra – reading it to me over the phone wasn't enough, of course) I would wait at the door to watch her pull up or run (yes run) to the door if I heard a car outside. I guess I just didn't want to miss a second of time which could have been spent looking at her. I really like looking at her. Cathy was feeling and doing the same type of things. We couldn't spend enough time with each other. I was only truly happy when she was close to me. That fact has never changed and it never will.

Cathy and I had, in the most natural way, formed a love for each other that was ready to burst but neither had expressed it yet. On New Year's Day 2011 Cathy came over to my house to spend a little time before leaving to visit her family in Canada. She had decided to stay in Canada if her feelings of love for me were not reciprocated. She would return to the U.S. if, however, we would be together. She and I, without saying it, felt the same way toward this hopeful relationship, to wit; we don't do casual. She asked me if there was more to our relationship than just being really good friends, as well as, Sandra's mom and dad.

Now, here's where I did a dumb thing. You see, I had written a letter to her expressing my love, dated and then sealed it. I planned to give to her in the future if the time seemed right and she returned to the USA, specifically the southern part of Indiana. I wasn't aware she planned to stay in Canada if our full relationship didn't take off. Instead of telling her there was indeed more, much more between us, (Dumb Move Alert) I got up and walked out of the room. Believe it or not, Cathy took this as a sign I wasn't interested in her. I returned with the letter before she made a mad dash to The Great White North. I gave it to her and she read it. Then, we both felt a weight lift off our shoulders (and our hearts) that left a feeling of joy no language can describe. There was also the realization we had finally found the one true love of our lives. We knew we could be completely honest with each other and completely trust each other. We had given up concern for ourselves and given it to each other. I do not have a single worry or concern for my wellbeing. That stopped the first time I heard Cathy say, "I love you." The same goes for her.

It didn't take us long (nanosecond is the correct term) to start looking for rings. We knew we would marry. We knew we needed rings. I knew a jeweler. The universe was in perfect alignment. All we needed was the jewelry store to open. Seriously, we would have said the "I dos" right then and there if a preacher or ship's captain had been standing in my living room at the time. Neither of them was, so we had to wait. Then, it was off to the "Wedding Bands Are Us" store.

Since the rings Cathy and I would be wearing were to be a symbol of our love and devotion, they had to be special – special and from a bona-fide jeweler – oh, and affordable too. Special, Check – From a jeweler, Check – Affordable, as it turns out, white gold is more expensive than yellow gold. How weird is that?

We went to a jeweler who has become a friend of ours, Jeff Ellis. Jeff is head honcho of Ellis Jewelers in Seymour, Indiana. He had a lot of rings for us to choose from. I watched Cathy look at ladies' rings and saw the one I thought had that certain special quality. I didn't indicate in any way which one I liked. It was going to be on her finger so she alone would decide. She picked the exact ring I had my eye on. Wait, it gets better. Now it was time for me to look at rings for dudes. Again, our buddy Jeff had plenty to choose from. I looked while Cathy secretly chose the one she liked best. Without any Jedi mind trickery, I picked the exact ring she had her eye on. They had to be sized and engraved so we didn't get them that day. They'd be ready in a couple weeks. Oh, by the way, Cathy's says, "U ARE MY WORLD" and mine says, "YOU HAVE MY HEART." Cool huh?

This is the day Cathy and I picked out our wedding rings. What a wonderful day it was.

Cathy did indeed see her family for about a month. In her absence I did a few minor things. Since we knew we were going to tie the knot sometime when she got back, I did wedding stuff. Let's see, I ordered her bouquet and my boutonniere, designed and ordered the cake (and had it stored in the restaurant's refrigerator where we would eat after the ceremony – she didn't know we'd have cake), made reservations for the dinner itself, picked up the rings and made many nervous phone calls to ensure all the ceremony details were ready, that is, the Mayor of Seymour, IN. would be available at our schedules 15-minute time slot; more about that in a bit.

During this time, I also worked on the proposal. I could have said the normal stuff like, how she would make me the happiest man on earth and I don't want to spend my life without her and all that jazz. I did, actually, but I did it while speaking the

Cathy and I with Jeff Ellis, aka, "Jeff the Jeweler" in 2017 at his store in Seymour, IN. Jeff is great man and a fantastic jeweler. You should stop by and see him some time.

language of love, French. I had never spoken French before. I never had a reason to. Now I did. I wrote the proposal on a piece of paper and gave it, along with a mini tape recorder, to the French teacher I worked with. She translated the lovey-dovey written English into le lovey-le dovey spoken French. I spent the time Cathy was gone listening to and repeating the proposal until I was confident-ish I had it memorized-ish.

Cathy finally returned from Canada. I met her at a restaurant with a single white rose in my grasp. I gave it to her and planted a mega-kiss upon her beautiful face. Then, we ate. Then, we left. We got back to my house to visit and that's when I sprang into action. I had a dozen red roses waiting for her on the kitchen table. She saw them – she liked them – flower mission accomplished. I was on a roll people. Cathy was standing in the living room. I approached her and knelt down on one slightly arthritic knee. I felt no pain. I presented her the engagement ring, took a deep breath, said a plethora of prayers, looked into her gorgeous eyes and spoke French.

I really needed those prayers to work and my pronunciation to be perfect since, Cathy speaks French! If she didn't, I could have ordered a cheeseburger and fries and she wouldn't have been the wiser. When I had finished, she smiled. Then, she said that all important word that made the 6 million times I rewound that tape worth it; she said, yes! Let the mega-kissing begin!

We got married on February 22, 2011 in a conference room just off the Mayor's office. Who cares that we weren't in a church or fancy shmancy resort? We were there to get hitched – he had the legal authority to hitch us – it worked out perfectly. After the hitching, we went to Appleby's© for the post-wedding feast. Cathy and I had our first date there (first table on the left, just past the greeter). My parents and Sandra were at our ceremony. Sandra had gotten leave from the USAF which made it extra special.

"We do" A little hamming it up for the camera after the individual I Dos were said.

We sat at a large corner booth and everything went great, with the possible exception of Sandra not realizing the flowers on top of the cake were plastic, not icing. She probably wouldn't want me to tell you that, so don't mention it if you see her.

A little cake (literally) after the post wedding feast at Applebee's, February 22, 2011.

    Cathy and I know we love each other and are completely devoted. Nothing in life is complete without us being together. We all know couples who don't seem to like being together. They gripe about one another or do things separately that they could do as a couple. Maybe we're weird or something, but we don't want alone time. We want us time, together, with each other, at the same time. If that's means we have a weird marital relationship, so be it.

    Cathy and I laugh, a lot. We have lots of inside jokes and catch phrases. We finish each other's sentences and have the same things on our minds all the time. These little things keep us close. Sometimes we laugh so hard, for so long, we have to call a truce so we can breathe again. Man, that's some fun stuff! If you're in a relationship, you should try it.

I'm a lucky man. Cathy loves to cook and bake and cover edible goodies (like these strawberries) in chocolate! Yes, very lucky indeed.

Cathy and I at Banker's Life Fieldhouse in Indianapolis after our first of eight performances (2014 - 2017) for the Indiana High School Boys' Basketball Championships.

Cathy as "Tigger" and me as Henry Hobo on the Disney Dream cruise ship. It was a Halloween themed cruise so everyone got to dress up one day at sea. When Cathy and I started dancing in the main lobby to the live music being performed, the whole lobby joined us. What a great time.

Husband and Wife and Best Friends! This photo was taken after a school basketball game on our wedding anniversary. The Color Guard bought us tickets to see Journey. Life doesn't get any better than this.

Cathy and I have found it impossible to even describe the love we have for each other. There are no words to accurately express it. It's the most overwhelming feeling we've ever had and it all started with a question about a Color Guard.

My beautiful, loving, intelligent and talented wife. The reason I'm happy.

My Baby Girl!

Section 8: Surface Decisions (Emotions)

Emotional decisions many times involve the surface of a situation not the deep reasons for the situation existing in the first place. More decisions will need to be made if only the surface is covered.

If a long-term relationship is what you want, deciding on who the relationship will be with should be made after a long enough evaluation period. You need to be with that person for a while to see what they're like during sports seasons, holidays, special occasions, boring occasions, the ever-inevitable relationship "rut," in sickness and in health, you get the idea.

By the way; it's Ok to get into a rut. It's how (or if) you get out of it that matters. The rut is always lurking about trying to slow things down. By the time you notice it, it's been there for a while. Once noticed, the rut must be addressed.

Good news time. Getting out of the rut is always a good thing and can be exciting, fulfilling, eye opening and a boost to your relationship. If, unfortunately, a rut can be stronger than your relationship, you need to find that out before you make a deep, heart saturated and legal commitment to another person.

For example; ladies if you choose a guy for his muscular physique and nice car, he may be only that. He may not be able or willing to add you equally to his life. You may find he's all biceps, pecks and pistons with not much else to offer. Gentlemen, you may find her gorgeous with great fashion sense and a cute, uhm, laugh. You may find out, however, she's high maintenance and must be the center of attention or she changes into someone far less attractive. She'll have the same fashion sense but she won't be laughing. She may try to control you with her looks and the fact other guys want to be with her. Yep, time to run like mad. The muscles and looks are on the surface. The true person is on the inside. Looks will fade, cars will rust and fashions will change. Don't bet your decision on them.

A thought for the ladies; a great looking, muscular, mysterious guy with a cool car may be a creep on the inside. An average looking, out of shape, bland guy driving an older car may be a true gentleman and not only knows how to treat a lady but wants to make her the focal point of his life. After all, he can always start working out.

Section 9: Taking Turns (Don't)

While playing most games, you take turns. Each player has an even amount of attempts to achieve success. An argument isn't a game. A screaming match doesn't produce real success. The one who screams the loudest or screams last may think they've won but they're wrong. Even if they get their way, they've still lost – their dignity.

Try this out the next time you feel your blood boil and you want to rip someone to shreds with your adrenalin charged, possibly profanity laced point of view. Don't. Don't take your next turn during the argument.

Let the other(s) say all they want without interruption. When they're done, wait. Believe me, they'll gladly take your turn and keep going. Once round two or three or 24 are finished, wait. Eventually, the opposing party will ask why you aren't arguing or why you're not saying anything. At that point, it's your turn.

You might say something like; you want to hear everything they have to say first before you respond or that you just don't want to argue, but talk. Follow that with, you're glad they told you what they did because you now have a better understanding of how they feel. They may interrupt so let them and then wait. When they stop again (if they ever do), you may continue.

The point is, don't take your turn in an argument. It keeps the argument going. Let them argue if they must but don't you be a part of it. Instead, try your best to stay calm, speak rationally and make real points about how you truly feel, not just the opposite view of what they've just said.

But how do you keep your blood pressure below ten thousand psi when they're screaming at you, calling you all sorts of horrible names? Try hard to understand they are hurt. So are you. The goal of all this is to relieve the hurt. Maybe, if you stay calm and rational enough you can heal some of that hurt. Not just for yourself but for them as well. That is what you really want deep down inside isn't it? It takes a strong you not to take your turn while being blasted, especially if the blaster is close to you; but wait you must.

If you want a chance to talk (not argue), heal the hurt (not cause more), and get your relationship back on track (no matter how far off it's been): control yourself and wait for the right time to take your turn.

Section 10: No Company (Better than Bad Company)

Some people feel they absolutely must be in a relationship. If not, something must be wrong with the cosmos. They go from one failed relationship to another without enough of a break to properly evaluate what went wrong and why. Many relationships start with a similar type person because they long for familiarity and a hope the new person will be better than the last.

We need time off between relationships so we don't rebound into the same old problems. We need time to look at ourselves to see if we've changed. Maybe, what we really want in a relationship has shifted a bit or we've identified new deal breakers. We may need to look at just how fast and far we are willing to go once our next relationship takes off.

Don't look so hard for a relationship, it will find you. Don't worry how long it takes either. It's better to wait than to go through another slow, agonizing relationship death; you know, when you ride in the car listening to your own music, eat at restaurants not talking much but spending most of your time just looking around (at other couples wondering if they're looking around for the same reason you are) or going to movies a lot because it blows a couple hours and you don't have to pay attention to each other. The list goes on.

I'm not saying a new relationship which comes around right after you're freed from the last one is automatically going to be bad. I'm just saying, take it easy on yourself and don't purposely go out looking for a new one. There are people out there looking for just that, a person looking for a relationship who may still be hurting from the last one. They may not really be interested in a relationship with you. They're interested in what they can get out of you while you think you have a relationship with them. They'll listen intently to you describe what went wrong with the last relationship and sympathize with you. They'll not make the same mistakes.

When they've gotten out of you all they want or find a more profitable person to join up with, they'll leave. You may find their debt is now yours and your heart is broken again.

This topic seems very negative but it doesn't have to be. Some say that time heals all wounds. Time can be a great healer of emotional wounds and give clarity to the one being healed. Don't allow yourself to be pushed into a new relationship by friends or family before you're ready. They're not going to be in it, you are.

You should always control the decisions of when, with whom, how fast and how far when it comes to your relationship.

Section 11: Broken (Together)

If you're in a relationship which seems broken or is breaking right before your eyes; listen to the song "Broken Together" by Casting Crowns. If you can, watch the video with the lyrics so you get the full meaning they have. It may help put into perspective, the pieces of your relationship which no longer fit properly. I sincerely hope it does.

Chapter 5: Listen Up, Men

Section 1: Her (Single Minded Obsession – Absolute Devotion – Pride – Protection – Love)

Obsess. Yes, I said obsess. Obsess over her happiness, health, safety, concerns, future, etc. not about yourself. The one who loves you should do the same for you. She will take better care of you than you will. We dudes cut corners; we don't eat properly, sleep enough, go to the doctor before we turn funny colors, take our medicine or exercise enough, if at all. She will, or at least she should, motivate us to do what must be done.

Take a hint man; show her you appreciate her efforts by doing what's necessary. If you concentrate on each other and not yourselves, you'll live better.

Take pride in talking about her whenever you can, after all, you should be her biggest fan. Make sure everyone knows you are the most blessed man on earth because she's yours. I'm telling you right now, my wife is so beautiful I wish I had more eyes.

Do you want to know what I hate? Ok, I'll tell you what I hate. I hate when so called "men" put down or make fun of the women they're with to other guys. It isn't funny at all. It shows a lack of appreciation and puts the guys who are laughing above her on the priority list. Joking around between couples is fun and understood. Making fun of her secretly proves the jerk doesn't want to get caught – because – he knows what he is saying will hurt her. He knows it will hurt her, but, he does it anyway, just not to her face. In my opinion (you just knew I'd give it didn't you), these cave men are simply cowardly, idiotic, childish, ungrateful boys, not men. They should all be single.

I also hate the Cro-Magnon references like, nice story Babe, now make me a sandwich. Those guys should starve. To those knuckle draggers I say, if you want a sandwich, ask her if she wants one first, then drag your lazy carcass to the kitchen and make her a sandwich – first, then make yourself one. Clean up your mess when you're done you pig!

Hint: If you're hungry, maybe she is too; ask her. If she says she'll make them for both of you or just you if she's not hungry, cool. All I'm saying is ask, then do, then clean up your mess.

It's simple guys; love her more than you need her.

Section 2: Where have the gentlemen gone? (Man Skills 101 – Don't forget to teach the boys.)

What is a gentleman? I read a dictionary definition which used terms like civilized, educated, sensitive and well-mannered to describe such a creature. Sounds nice enough but how does that apply to us? Lets' break it down, shall we? We shall.

Civilized: We're all civilized enough not to be put in a zoo, so let's move on. Educated: You're reading this book so your brain cells have been and are now being exercised. Good enough. Now we come to the main points; being sensitive and well-mannered.

Sensitive: Watch what you say and do to her and about her. Watch her reaction to what you say and do to her and about her. If her reactions are good, you've done well. If her reactions are bad, pack your crap and move into the dog house buddy. If her bad reactions surprise or confuse you, you obviously haven't been sensitive (receptive) to her emotions.

Speaking of being receptive; the better the phone or radio reception is, the better the understanding of what's being heard, read or seen. You must be receptive to what she says and does to have a better understanding of her. I've said this many times; I didn't marry Cathy to ignore her. I married her to be her husband, you know, the person who knows her best.

Sensitive also involves your soft approach when she is emotionally hurting. If something is upsetting her she needs you to comfort her. I don't care how big and burly you may be, she needs you. She loves you for all your big burliness so love her back with the sensitivity she needs. Being strong is one thing. Being strong enough to be gentle is a talent.

Being Well-Mannered: Don't whine, it's not gonna kill ya. What does "well-mannered" mean exactly? It means different things to different people but I know what not being well-mannered looks, sounds and unfortunately smells like, and so do you. Body sounds and smells may have been funny when you were young (I didn't understand it then and still don't) but not anymore.

Being well-mannered is simple; be courteous, kind, thoughtful, generous and anything else that will make her smile, blush and drool over you. While you're being well-mannered, don't forget to be masculine and strong, oh yeah, and helpful with a sense of humor too. See, it's simple. Simple my pa-tooty. Simple or not, do it.

Back to reality. Being a well-mannered dude is as easy as this; have her on your mind when you're doing things. If you want a light snack or an XL double pepperoni pizza with extra sauce and triple cheese, see if she wants something to eat as well. Introduce her to everyone who hasn't had the good fortune to meet her yet. Open doors for her (including car doors - wait until she sits, pull out the seat belt and hand it to her then gently close her door), help her with her coat, pull out her chair at restaurants, ask her what she'd like to have, then, order for her with a phrase like "My lovely wife would like the XL double pepperoni pizza with extra sauce and triple cheese please and I'll just have a salad." I know it's not proper to make personal comments because I'm writing this to you readers, but I just re-read that last sentence and could visualize it in my mind – my side kinda hurts from laughing.

Hold her hand while you're waiting for your food. Look at her when she's talking to you. Look at her when you're talking to her. My wife told me something shortly after we got together. She told me one of the things that made her feel close to me was that I looked at her when she spoke. I've always remembered that. Compliment how nice she looks and be specific. Compliment her hair, eyes, clothes, shoes, perfume and so on. Dude, she makes you look good, don't forget that.

You, Sir, are an important person. You're interesting with many things on your mind. That's just great. Now put a sock in it for a while and ask her how her day went. Ask her how her week went while you're at it and add what she's thinking about concerning the future. She wants to know how you are as well but we men types tend to either talk about ourselves too much or hardly talk at all. Have a conversation with her and let her have the majority of the time. You may find out things you didn't know. Scratch that. You will find out things you didn't know. It's good to know things, especially about her. What she tells you will be important to her and should be to you.

Here's a difficult one. Ask her if there's anything you could do better concerning your relationship. She'll ask the same of you. Open your conversation to the deep feelings you have for each other. Let it out. You may end up much closer to each other mentally, emotionally and yes, physically. Good stuff, man.

I think about the sentinels (guards) at the Tomb of the Unknown Soldiers. They carry a rifle with fixed bayonet and maneuver them with such control and grace. They wear immaculate uniforms and walk without the slightest bounce as if they were floating just above the ground. The rifle movements and walk look effortless but it takes strength and concentration.

They say very little except to pass on and acknowledge their orders, however, if anyone shows disrespect at the tomb, the sentinel will stop, face the disrespectful person and issue a loud, aggressive warning while having placed their rifle in a defensive position. They are not putting on a show or joking. They are completely serious.

Once the atmosphere returns to its proper reverence, the sentinel also returns to their duty. I think being a gentleman is something like that. Being strong but not having that as you're only noticeable trait, being graceful (sensitive and well-mannered) while not diminishing your masculinity, and (this is where true strength comes in) not compromising the integrity of your relationship in the same way the sentinel will not compromise the reverence mandatory for our nations most hallowed ground.

Don't forget to teach the boys. Teach the boys what? Here's a list; how to tie a neck tie, shine their (and yours, and everybody else's) shoes, shave without hemorrhaging all over the bathroom, bathe their bods (not necessarily how, but do what it takes to make being clean of body, hair, ears, teeth, fingernails, etc. a normal part of their existence), the words "please," "thank you," "Sir" and "Ma'am," being able to patiently and quietly wait their turn, how not to interrupt others, how to speak to adults in a language closer to the adult's level, how to dress appropriately for different occasions (wedding, funeral, nice dinner out, family photos, school, holidays, church, etc.). A variety of clothes is necessary to accomplish this.

As for you, you don't want to be seen next to your lady in her stunning (good word to use) outfit while you're sporting a t-shirt and jeans. It's a nice t-shirt (I get it) but it doesn't fit the occasion. You love the jeans because they don't ride up your great divide into your nether region but they still aren't right for the occasion. Teach the boys these lessons and be the example for them to follow and you'll have young men on your hands before you know it.

A thought about neck ties; a lot of guys say they don't like wearing them. I don't get it. The tie isn't around your neck, the shirt collar is. You don't actually feel the tie at all. If you don't like wearing a tie, loosen your shirt collar a little or just buy shirts with a bigger collar. It's sometimes fashionable to wear the collar unbuttoned with the tie knot loosened, even in a suit. Well, that about solves the "I don't like wearing a tie" problem pretty well, now doesn't it?

Hint: A pair of black slacks, black dress shirt and black dress shoes can work wonders. The shirt can be worn tucked in or left out, the sleeves can be down or rolled partially up and it works with or without a tie. It's slimming too, if you need that. Basic black attire, nice cologne, decent hair and some manners – man, you will make her happy and proud to show you off.

That's a home run, touchdown, and gold medal all rolled into one!

Section 3: Superheroes (Like Us)

Get Ready – Brace for Impact – Here It Comes: When it comes to her, you are everything. At least you're supposed to be. You should want to be.

When we were kids, most of us wanted to be superheroes. We wanted super powers, super gadgets, super costumes and someone to show off to. Well, congratulations Mister, you got your wish. No, you won't get the standard issue super powers like incredible strength or the ability to fly. Nope, no car or utility belt (you may have a ring on your finger though– that's pretty super). I'm not talking make believe here. You are her superhero, so show off.

The world can be mean sometimes. It can cause her to feel sad, angry and helpless. Be her shield. Be the one who takes the hits. Stand in front of her and stand firm. You may be knocked around, bruised and battered by the world but every mark on you is a mark you protected her from. Be her rock, unmovable, solid and strong. When she feels she's being pulled here and there, be her anchor. Hold her close, don't let her go. Nothing bad can reach her unless it gets past you and nothing gets past you!

That's what superheroes do. Superheroes protect others, sometimes at their own expense. Why do we do this; because we are men; we are boyfriends, fiancé's and husbands - superheroes.

Section 4: Sheep, Wolves and Sheep Dogs (Hint: You should be the Sheep Dog, not the Wolf)

Sheep go around all day pretty much in a daze with their heads down; eat a little grass here, eat a little grass there, stand over here, no wait, over there, Baa, Baa, Baa. They don't notice much. The dangers surrounding and closing in on the sheep are a non-issue to the future sweaters since they're too busy being sheep. Most people are sheep.

Wolves hunt sheep. Wolves hunt sheep for their money, bodies, emotions and anything else they can take. Wolves keep their heads low trying to blend into the background but their eyes fixed on the sheep. They move carefully, not drawing attention to themselves until they're close enough to strike. Sometimes, the wolf puts on "sheep's clothing" to get even closer, fooling the sheep and gaining their trust, then, the kill.

Sheep Dogs spend their days close to the sheep but focused on the wolves. Their heads are up with their eyes scanning for wolves. Sheep Dogs will maneuver to stay in a direct line with a wolf. This ensures the fastest interception possible should the wolf attack. At the point of interception, the wolf is decimated. The Sheep Dog is the protector of the sheep. The sheep don't always appreciate the Sheep Dog's rules but the Sheep Dogs know things the sheep do not – maybe it's better that way.

All I know is, men must be vigilant for the wolves of this world. We must look for them, not just react when they strike. It's said the best defense is a good offense. Yep.

Sheep: Your loved ones - *Wolves:* Problematic Humans, Con Men/Women, Scam Artists, Thieves, Liars, Bullies, Molesters, Rapist, Murderers - *Sheep Dogs:* You and I

Section 5: Macho Man (I hope you're not)

What is "macho" exactly? Men have been led to believe by movies, T.V., music and their buddies it consists of being a loud, obnoxious, foul mouthed, sexist, flexing, pile of nearly visible testosterone.

I read a dictionary describe macho as "characteristics manifested in an assertive (Ok), self-conscious (Huh?) or dominating (No Way) way. It also said, "an exaggerated sense of power or (hold on to something) "the right to dominate." I am not kidding. So being a macho man means being a pushy, egotistical, tyrant with a self-righteous sense of power over others, predominately women. Well, I think not. I'll bet that came as no surprise.

If you must be overtly macho for some reason, try being assertive with your praise about your lady's accomplishments, self-conscious of your words and actions that they're always for her benefit and being the dominant protective force around her.

You can exercise and be a physical beast (she may like that) and be direct, focused and always ready to make decisions (she may like that too) but, that gives you no rights whatsoever to dominate her or anyone else. People should follow leaders because they want to not because they have to.

Macho should mean your assertiveness, self-consciousness (self-evaluation) and dominate personality is shown in good leadership of yourself first. Others may follow your example but they should do so by their own choice, not by your right to force it upon them – which you don't have.

The military loves acronyms. They'll acronym anything they can get their hands on. They try hard to make them sound cool, too. Our base Special Weapons and Tactics (SWAT) team's name was changed several times. First it was Emergency Services Team (EST), then Emergency Response Team (ERT), then Tactical Response Team (TRT), then back to one of the former names. I heard of a base that had actually named theirs the Tactical Neutralization Team or (TNT). I have one for M.A.C.H.O. (Men Always being Caring and Honest to Others). Catchy? Probably not, but it sends the right message.

Section 6: The Pedestal (Hi Babe!)

I adore my wife. I not only love her but I am in love with her, so I put her on a preverbal pedestal. I've lifted her to an elevated level and placed her above all others. I want my "Baby Girl" as I like to call her (and she likes to be called) to know by my words, emotions and actions exactly how I feel about her. She is the only one. She alone is on the pedestal.

Come on guys, this isn't difficult if you not only love but are in love with your lady. I'm talking about heart pounding, chest thumping, shout it from the mountain tops in love. It's masculine to be in love. It's also masculine to show it.

I want my wife to have the best of everything, not just the best stuff, but my best. Everyone knows how good a cook she is, because I tell them. Everyone knows how talented and intelligent she is, because I tell them. There's no doubt in anyone's mind how I feel toward my wife. That's the way it's supposed to be, if you not only love, but are in love with your lady.

I mentioned earlier that Cathy is originally from Canada. A little while after we were married she started the process to become a US citizen. Let me tell you, it's quite a process; over $700.00 dollars, tons of paperwork, an interview and a test. We had to travel over an hour south of where we lived for one part of the process, then travel over an hour north for another. Oh yeah, your appointments are set in stone. If you miss one, you may have to start the entire process over again. No refund, of course.

It was stressful but Cathy got though it with flying colors, even acing the test. One of the proudest moments of my life was seeing her raise her hand and recite the oath of citizenship. On June 18, 2014 she became a proud new American!

Cathy's US citizenship swearing in ceremony on June 18, 2014 at the US Immigration Office in Indianapolis. It was a long road to this moment but well worth it.

Congratulations to my wonderful wife, and brand new American!

This is one of the t-shirts I designed for Cathy after she received her citizenship. I like to call her my "Americanadian." I'm so very proud of her.

I try hard to pay attention to her in stores to see what items she picks up and admires. If I get the feeling she'd like it for some future gift giving occasion, I secretly get it and store it under the bed in the "no looky" zone. By the way; that is the only type of secret I'll keep from my wife.

I tell my wife I love her all the time. It takes place a few times a day in fact. No, it doesn't grow old. Growing old is what I want to do with her. I'll be telling her in words, love letters, poems, cards and shouts from the mountain tops how much I love her. Pay attention here. I do this, not because I feel obligated to do so, but because I consider her the reason I'm happy. I'm happy because she loves me. How could I do anything less for the woman who loves me? I won't do less but I'll try to do more.

Ok, where is all this going? Am I saying you should pamper your lady all the time like painting her finger and toe nails, buying her certificates for massages and facials, stuff like that? Should you go out of your way to give her everything she wants? Do you have to say I love you every day and write love letters to her and all that mushy stuff? Wake up men, yes! Why wouldn't you? Seriously, why wouldn't you? Got any answers? If you do, you're selfish. Oh, yes you are. Ok, maybe you're self-conscience or embarrassed instead. If you're selfish, get out of the relationship. She deserves better. If you're self-conscience or embarrassed, get over it before she gets over you.

There's a misconception about men out there. It says men don't cry, cuddle, say I love you over the phone with the same volume as the rest of the conversation (mumbling is the usual way), wear pink, write mushy love letters and so on. It's widely believed men should act like their relationship is a burden or threat to their masculinity. No doubt a "man" or "men" derived this pile of poopy to mask their own immature weaknesses.

Yeah, I said it, immature and weak. A man who won't openly show his emotions toward his lady is weak in my opinion. It takes no effort to do nothing, that's easy. It takes effort to do something, even if that something is as simple as saying three words loud enough to sound like you mean them.

I'm a man in love with a woman. I can cry for and with her because I'm a man. I cuddle with her because, well, it feels great and I'm a man. I say, write and text I love you to her because I'm a man, her man. I wear my tie with pink in it (to remember my granddaughter who passed away) because I'm a man and I write love letters and poems (remember, they don't have to rhyme – I hope) to her because I am a man. Men should do these things.

Your lady should be on a pedestal in your heart. She must be the only one there. No other person or thing (sports, buddies, motorcycles, hunting seasons, etc.) should be in competition with her. She is your lady, you are her man. Build her a pedestal.

Section 7: Because it's Wednesday (or whenever)

Holidays are great, aren't they? Yes, they are. They're predictable though. It seems like every year about the same time, they show up again. Women love getting flowers. Women get flowers on holidays. Women get flowers on predictable holidays, the same times each year like clockwork. Not bad. Not good either.

First of all, women want and deserve flowers. Second, women notice when flowers aren't given at the predictable times (Valentine's Day, Mother's Day, their birthday, wedding anniversary, etc.). Third, women would like flowers at other times. If not, they only receive them say, five times a year at best.

Each year has at least 365 days in it. That means she goes without getting flowers approximately 360 days out of the year. Ok, add a full two weeks per flower arrival for how long they stay nice enough to display. That adds up to 10 weeks (70 days) out of 52 weeks (365 days) that she's reminded, via colorfully topped plant life, that you were thinking about her. Oh, but remember, this is only on those predictable holidays or special occasions. A full 42 weeks (294 days) out of the year she's left without the little pollen bombs she loves so much. Does that sound right to you? Answer: Big fat no.

Yesterday morning, before I wrote some of the text for the "Her" topic, I called a florist and ordered flowers for my wife. They were delivered about 10am at her work. It was a Wednesday. A non-holiday Wednesday with no special meaning attached to it, until the flowers arrived. Get the picture? It was a simple gesture with a clear meaning, that being, I'm thinking of you and I love you. The card delivered with the flowers simply read "Because it's Wednesday."

Of course, you don't have to send flowers. You could send chocolates. You actually don't have to send anything. Figure out what would make her day and do it at unpredictable times. It's actually fun and the rewards you reap can be – I'll let your imagination handle that one.

Example: Cook (not microwaving) dinner. Don't forget dessert. It should go without saying the dinner and dessert should be her favorites. If you're thinking, dude, I don't cook – why in the name of lasagna don't you? You mean she has to cook every meal for you (and your kids) without a break? That's not fair. Learn to cook a few things. The kitchen isn't a scary place. It's a nice place where the food is! Grab a cook book and start reading. Better yet, ask her to teach you. You get to be in the kitchen with her while she shows you how to cook food you also get to eat. This is a good thing guys. Being able to help her, learning a new skill, eating the food = zero dollars – Spending time with her = Priceless.

Section 8: Male vs Men (Polar Opposites)

WARNING: The following contains some sweeping generalities. This was done on purpose so don't get your boxers in a bind. Grab a sense of humor and read on.

I've touched on this a little already but here are thirteen more points to wrap your gray matter around.

1) Men (males who actually act like men) Males (men who actually don't)

2) A man has strong character – a male may or may not have strong muscles.

3) Strong character is harder to achieve and maintain than strong muscles.

4) Men are not afraid of their emotions; males are terrified by the thought of being sensitive or tender.

5) A male in "men's clothing" will not have read this far; they'll have gotten ticked off, said "I don't need this" or "this is stupid" or "this guy is stupid" or "stupid, stupid, stupid" or something else enlightening and tossed this book away. Congratulations on still being here.

6) A man is considerate, compassionate, complimentary and caring (all while tearing down and re-building an engine and simultaneously barbequing a rattle snake he killed with his bare hands over a fire he made with his own arm pit hair and gasoline; grunt, grunt, snort, snort, scratch, scratch).

7) Men accept and fulfill their responsibilities as best they can. Males reject most of their responsibilities. The responsibilities they can't get away from are given as little effort as possible; any more effort and it might encroach into video game time, sleep time, computer time, buddies time, beer time and any other excuse they can conjure up not to be men.

8) Men ask for directions (even from women) because they don't like being lost and feeling embarrassed. Being lost interferes with getting things done and feeling embarrassed is embarrassing. Males won't ask for directions because they think it's somehow a sign of weakness. What? Being lost and not asking for direction is a sign of weakness, dude.

Hint: Being lost is not a sign of weakness. It means at some point, between where you started and where you were when you realize something was terribly wrong, you made at least one wrong turn. It's just a directional oops. Correct the oops and press on.

If you feel embarrassed because you're lost and don't ask for directions, you'll stay lost and embarrassed longer. Of course, none of this is a concern if you have a navigation system, right? Yeah, those things never send you down a one-way street to nowhere or the back loading docks of an airport when you're looking for a hospital do they?

9) A man can speak in public; a toast at a party or prayer before a meal. A man can even speak at emotionally difficult times like giving the eulogy at a funeral. That can be tough but a man will do it. A male, no way.

10) A man protects their immediate family members: see Chapter 5, Section 5 "Superheroes like us." Sometimes, a man has to protect family members from each other; see, Chapter 6, Section 4, "Being a part or being apart." A male will protect their interests and little else.

11) Men will follow the advice of ZZ Top when they sing "Every girl's crazy 'bout a sharp dressed man." They'll wear something totally uncomfortable, too hot, too formal, restrictive and yucky, just to look sharp for their lady. A male might wash (or have their lady wash) their t-shirt before wearing it, again, but only if it really, really doesn't pass the sniff test.

12) Men change diapers. Males cry like the baby with the poop slathered butt trying to get out of it. If you're a male and the child is yours, that's your poop encrusted son or daughter's butt that needs to be cleaned, soothed with lotion and covered with a fresh diaper. They need you. They can't do it themselves. Their delicate skin will get a rash (or worse) if the copious amounts of liquid and solid toxic mortar isn't gently removed from their cute little pa-tooty. Be a man and clean that poop!

13) This probably should have been number one; a man is male in gender; a male is not necessarily a man in action.

Chapter 6: The Home

Section 1: Ownership (It belongs to you, not your kids.)

The only place where we have the possibility of real "say so" is in our own home, apartment, cave or whatever we cop-a-squat in. If you own it or are making the payments, you have the say as to what can and cannot happen there. Those living with you are subject to the awesome power you possess as chief decision maker. This power is bestowed upon you by an age-old understanding. That being; if I'm forking over the money for this place, it's gonna run the way I want it to.

The home is usually the largest financial investment a person can make. That thought alone puts the power of decision making squarely in the lap(s) of those carrying the financial burden. In other words, it's yours. You can decide anything you want – you and no one else. Feel better?

If your kids want to have a say in a particular matter concerning your largest financial investment, figure how much it's worth and charge them to get their way (only if you agree). Let's say they want to paint their room neon purple, $200.00. They can mow yards, wash cars or whatever to raise the money. It will teach them a good lesson.

By the way, the less you like their idea (but are still willing to let it happen) the more it costs them. This isn't only for decisions about the home as a building. It also covers activities or behavior related to living there. Let's hit the most common ones.

Curfews: Curfews are notoriously disagreed upon by parents and their kids. The curfew should have a smaller "pm" number the younger the kids are, ex: fifteen-year-olds have a smaller "pm" number than eighteen-year-olds. Fifteen-year-olds back by, oh let's say, 8pm and eighteen-year-olds by 11pm; whatever numbers work for you. I said you, not them.

There are different priorities in the decision-making process for parents and kids and they don't mix well. If your kid shows maturity beyond their years, great. What about their friends? After all, your child's elevated maturity level can be trumped by the smile of a humanoid of the opposite sex. It takes about a second and a half.

Look, you worry about your kid's safety and adult development. Your kids worry about their popularity status and personal drama quotient. See, they don't mix. If, however, you like their friends (it's possible), maybe give them a little slack. If they don't say thank you or if they come back one nanosecond late, lock 'em in their room for good, hee, hee.

Dating: The things your child will want to date will seem strange to you. That was a little harsh, wasn't it? Sorry. Our granddaughter is a beautiful girl. I like the t-shirt which expressed the worldwide fact that guns don't kill people, dads of pretty daughters do. Fact: Parents often don't like the person their child wants to date. Fact: Children want to date. Fact: Parents must profile the person their child wants to date. Fact: Children can just get over it.

Your child should understand you look at their date through a different set of eyes, expectations and standards. When, not if, you meet and talk with them, their attire, manners (if any), language, slang, odor and perceived personality will be scrutinized by you and you alone will make the ultimate decision of whether or not the date commences. If they (your child) don't understand this, they're too young and or immature to date; keep 'em home. That'll take care of a large percent of the problem. If you child pitches a fit, tell them to blame me. If they pitch a fit, they're too young and or immature to date. If they blame me, they're too young and or immature to date.

Seriously, you want your child to meet people, date and have fun. They need this to grow as a person. But, your child is going to be alone with their date for hours. Your child is not ready to be alone with anyone unless they fully understand your concerns. That's a part of their maturity growth. Your feelings are motivated by love. Their understanding of your feelings should be motivated by their love of your love for them.

Fashion: Most often the problem with teen fashion isn't necessarily what something looks like but how little of it there is. I'm a child of the late 70s and early 80s. Late 70s fashions were cool then and still are. The 80s had fashions that were mostly mistakes. Just how many polo shirts with the collars turned up can a guy wear at one time, anyway? Leg warmers, why? Ok, Ok, parachute pants were awesome.

Back to today. If you as a parent (and owner of the home) don't agree with a piece of clothing, for any reason, don't allow it in your house. If your child (with their own money) buys something you obviously don't approve of (they know what your reaction will be, believe me) have them return it and get their money back. If they used your money, have them return it and give you your money back. You'll probably have to go with them on their fashion hunt. Remember, if they pitch a fit they're too young and or immature to do this on their own.

Modesty sends a clear message. So does a middle school girl with a push up bra, a V-neck t-shirt two sizes too small over a pair of shorts cutting off blood flow to her legs with a 1 inch tall zipper. It's up to you as parents to control (yes, I said control) what is worn by your daughters, period! They don't understand how many wolves might be watching them.

Boys don't show off the way girls do. They seem to like suggestive graphics on their shirts. Have them read what their shirt says to grandma. Better yet, have grandma read it out loud to them. Those graphics sound really creepy when recited by a 60 or 70-year-old woman.

Bottom line; there are infinite ways your kids can be on the cutting edge of fashion. They should enjoy their generation's style, but not at the expense of your family name, reputation or your personal preferences as the ones who provide them shelter.

Section 2: The Lord giveth and the Lord taketh away. (So can you)

If your kid won't take out the trash but constantly plays their (your) video game system – throw it (not them) in the trash. You could sell the thing and use the money to pay a neighbor kid to take your trash to the curb. Your kid loses the game system and a neighbor kid who's not even related to you (but has a better work ethic and maturity level than your kid) gets paid. Your house doesn't have trash piling up, the neighbor kid is happy and you don't have to hear the sounds of the underworld or some other universe being attacked all day. Better yet, take the system, sell it and buy yourself something nice. I personally like that one. This is done, of course, after you've reminded them about the trash over a length of time. Kids forget (so do we) but there comes a time when they aren't forgetting, they're ignoring.

True story. This is about me and electricity; actually, it's about me wasting electricity. When I was a mere teen I had a "habit" of leaving my bedroom light on when I'd go somewhere. My mom first responded to this error in my judgment by shutting it off herself (a few times). After a few times came and went, she told me to go back to my room and shut it off. After a while of doing that, she decided one day not to tell me to go back and just let me go wherever I was going without the slightest interruption.

Yes, there's more. Once I had reached my destination, which was about 15 minutes from our house via the highway, she called for me; pre-cell phone days ya'll. I answered the phone wondering what could be wrong. She told me nothing was wrong but she needed me to come home right away. I said "see ya" to my friends, got in the car and went home. When I walked in our house my mom and dad were sitting on the couch watching TV. Mom casually looked up at me and simply said; "You left your room light on." That was it. I walked down the hall to my room, turned the light off and never forgot again.

There's a time for work and a time for play. Play should usually come after work. If the games aren't played, no harm is done. If the trash isn't taken out, the house stinks and flies and maggots move in. Gross. No video game is worth that. Plus, if the kid doesn't take the trash out (or whatever chore they have) without being told all the time - you guessed it - they're too young and or immature to operate the expensive video game system. You can invent new live action role playing games for them like "Trash Assassins," "Vacuum Rangers" or "Toilet Bowl Ninjas." They'll just love it.

Your kid's clothes are all over the floor, still? Warn them as many times as you want but when you feel they're ignoring you, toss them out or put them in the next yard sale and you keep the money. You may think, my kid will be naked within a month. I can't help you there.

Section 3: The Disappearing Act (How to keep your house clean.)

Is your kid's room (which you're paying for) a "pig pen?" Tell them to start cleaning it, now. Now is not defined as by the week end if it's Monday. Now is by the next time their heart beats again, aka, right this second! Everything stops in their life, no matter what it is (unless they want to take out the trash) and they start Olympic level room cleaning. Give the darlings a time limit to finish. If you don't, they won't. Tell them, when time is up anything on the floor goes out the door. That goes for anything not properly put away too. Have them pick up what's on the floor. Now, sell what you can and buy yourself something nice.

You can, of course, buy your kids educational stuff, underwear, yard care equipment or more deodorant, depending on the need. You may find your kids will ask if the things they no longer want can be sold and they keep the money. That's a cool idea. You want them to see that their things have value and it's ok to outgrow or just not want them. It's not ok, however, for those things to pollute your home. Magic ain't so hard after all.

Section 4: Being a part or being apart. (Family Survival)

What I'm about to say may shock some of you and anger others. It might motivate and strengthen a few as well. This is one of the most serious topics in this book. If you're facing the seemingly impossible task of dealing with a totally unruly member of your family, this topic is for you.

Let me start by saying this is about survival, specifically, family survival. When I say unruly, I mean just that; someone who refuses to abide by the rules. The rules I speak of are either your rules as parents and or the law. If they're repeatedly breaking rules without apology, excuse, explanation or remorse, they're doing so because they have lost all respect for you, your home and the law. They do not care one bit about how their behavior affects your emotions, relationships, finances, reputation or legal standing (see Problematic Humans).

They aren't living as a part of the family. In fact, they're probably tearing the family apart. I'm referring to persons (kids and adults) who are fully capable and intelligent enough to understand right from wrong and are choosing wrong on purpose; the 13-year-old who refuses to do homework or house work, bullies their siblings, yells and curses at you, breaks things in the home, stays out overnight without permission, smokes and drinks; the 17-year-old who threatens others in the family, hits their siblings, smokes dope and steals from you; the 21-year-old who won't get a job, has friends basically move in without your consent, is arrested and pleads with you to bail them out then acts like nothing happened (until they get arrested again). There are many descriptions I could give but I'm sure you understand my point.

Do you dread going home knowing they'll be there? Do you dread being home knowing they've just returned. Do you divide their chores between everyone else to avoid trying to get them to help? Have you hidden your jewelry, cash and personal belongings from them? Have they put a lock on their room's door or forbidden you to enter theirs but they have the run of the house? Do you give them money or things to appease them? Are you or others in your family scared of them? Has anyone in your family been abused by them? Do you feel the family would be better off with them living somewhere else? If you answered yes to any of these questions, its high time something was done.

Since they refuse to be a part of the family they need to be apart from the family. Yes, apart. If their behavior is destructive in any way (emotional, physical, psychological, financial) and they refuse to correct it, they need to go. If asking them to do or stop doing something makes them erupt like a volcano, or if making a decision without consulting them first results in your home and its occupants being in deep crap-oh-la, you have a serious problem and it has a name. If you can't even ask them a question or make a decision in your own home, they've taken your authority and your rights as the home owner away. They've also taken control of every one's life that lives there. They need to go.

When should this happen? The time frame is up to you. Only you know how long is too long to be dealing with this. Some won't tolerate this kind of inter-family terrorism for more than a few weeks; others go for years before they act.

What degree of apart are we talking about? I know a family who had two boys, one big and one small. The big kid was so big he not only bullied his brother but also hit his mom and dad a few times. After a couple intense skirmishes between the boys, their mother told the bigger brother she would call the police and have him arrested if he ever hit his smaller brother again. Guess what happened? The bigger brother hit the smaller brother again and mom called the police. The police arrived – mom explained the situation – the bigger brother was arrested. He stated in a shocked voice while in handcuffs on his way to the patrol car's back seat that he never thought she'd do it. His mom relied, "Have I ever lied to you before?" He admitted she hadn't. Mom added, "Then why would I start now?" He had no response. There's the key.

People like this don't think anything substantial or permanent will happen to them, so, why should they stop? There's something powerful about saying what you mean and meaning what you say. When others figure out you mean business, they may just start paying closer attention and heed your warnings.

There are programs for pre-teens and teens who are cancers in their own homes. Sending them to one of these programs may save them; that is what you really want. You're not turning your back on them or abandoning them; you are trying to save them from themselves. If they're 18 years old or older and are terrorizing anyone or any part of your life, tell them to move out immediately. You're trying to save them too.

When you've decided you've done enough talking, lecturing, pleading, screaming, crying, avoiding and living in fear; for the sake of the true family members, remove the offender. They are now apart from the family. Have the police there if you need to but remove them. You can negotiate their return on your terms if they stop behaving in the manner which caused their removal.

You may want to change the locks on your doors, put locking gas caps on your vehicles and tell your neighbors. They (the removed) will probably tell their friends you kicked them out; so what. They may ask you for money in a couple weeks. They won't ask how you or the family are doing. They'll just ask for (or demand) money. You can give it to them if you want. I certainly wouldn't. At some point they have to solve their own problems or they'll never grow up.

Remember one thing about your decision to safeguard your home. You were put in a position no one should ever be in. You endured and suffered because of their behavior. They didn't suffer at all. You were strong enough to act and you did the right thing. This whole thing was their fault, not yours. It's your home, not theirs.

Section 5: The Minimum Law (Everything else is conditional)

We all want lots and lots of stuff. We don't need lots and lots of stuff. We think we do, but we really don't. We need the minimum to make it in this life and we should have it. When we're on our own, everything we have is usually purchased with our hard-earned money. Our ability to purchase the stuff we want is conditional on our income which is conditional on us keeping a job. We work, we earn, we buy, we have. Goody for us.

Now for the kids. They need the minimum to make it and they should have it and more. In fact, they should get all kinds of stuff, lots and lots of stuff, but only if their behavior warrants it. If your work behavior is appropriate (being on time, doing the work required of you without blurting out smart-aleck comments) you'll continue being paid, ergo, you can buy more stuff. If your kid's behavior, not just at home but everywhere, is appropriate, then pile on the extra stuff. The extra stuff is conditional on their continued good behavior as defined by you. Easy, huh?

Now for the breakdown: Exceptional Behavior equals lots and lots of stuff beyond the minimum. Great Behavior equal lots of stuff beyond the minimum. Good Behavior equals some stuff beyond the minimum. Fair Behavior equals the minimum. Bad Behavior equals the minimum with corrective discipline. Horrible Behavior equals - See (*Being a part or being apart.*)

What is minimum stuff, anyway? I'd say it's a home with a bedroom (they may have to share), nutritional food and drink, enough clothing to cover their bods during all seasons (if you have them). I live in Indiana. We have seasons like really hot, really cold and both in the same day. My publisher and buddy from the USAF, Mark, aka: Mush (long story) lives in California. I think they have one season there. It's called, beautiful weather season.

Ok, back to the kid's clothes. This does not require buying 17 of everything or the slightest lean toward "popular" fashion trends. They need carcass cleaning supplies like soap, shampoo, deodorant (you can buy 17 of them just to be safe), tooth paste and brush and any other specific items for specific needs.

Notice I didn't say anything about name brands. Your budget will probably dictate what brands you buy. Oh yeah, you're buying it aren't you? Therefore, you can decide what you buy with your hard-earned money. You can get your kid the brands they want, but you don't have to.

I also didn't mention anything which contains a battery, has a charger, a connector, two-year service plan, controller, touch screen, interface, outerface, keyboard or the ability to entertain or communicate with the rest of the planet. They aren't necessary to protect, feed, clothe or clean your offspring. They are conditional.

If your kiddies already have those things, great. I hope they earned them by being mature and cooperative with you. I sincerely hope they weren't given those things to keep them from whining all over the place and making a mess of their dignity. If they have them now and their behavior is slipping, their extra stuff is in jeopardy. The more often and more severe the slip, the closer they get to the minimum. Their "job," if you will, is to continuously mature, be cooperative with you as their parent and provider and be appreciative for what they have; even if it's not the most recent invention from the Technology Gods on Mount Tweet.

The minimum law clearly states: The offspring of the parents shall be afforded the minimum necessary by law to sustain their lives and prevent them from stinking up the joint. The offspring shall conduct themselves in a manner, if they so choose, as to compel the parents to provide the offspring with lots and lots of stuff beyond the minimum. If said offspring fail to conduct themselves in this manner upon receipt of lots and lots of stuff, the aforementioned lots and lots of stuff, will be gone. (I've paraphrased the actual statute, of course)

Too many kids feel entitled to too much. They're not even paying for whatever they have. If you are, you decide what they get. Their behavior decides how long they keep it. Hey, whacha gonna do; it's the law.

Section 6: Spock (Vulcan Family Priorities)

If you're a fan of the original cast of *Star Trek* (and you should be) you'll be familiar with this idea. Mr. Spock said in one of the movies they made after the show was beamed off the air, that the needs of the many outweigh the needs of the few, or the one. It's true, but the degree of truth depends on your family's dynamics; ages, core personalities, fake personalities and such.

The family as a whole is the priority not a single individual. I'm not talking about those with real needs like a physical handicap or emotional problem. Those family members automatically receive help from the compassion and love of the family. I'm talking about the ones who receive unnecessary help or unfair advantages from a sense of fear or dread of what they might do if they don't get their way. I'm talking about those who thrive on making everyone else jump through their hoops or just plain jump when they pull one of their self-induced, fake steak and phony bologna temper tantrums. I want to "talk" to them right now; the one who believes the family exists just for them. You'll have to interrupt their important endeavors and put the book right in front of their face. Ready, good. Let me at 'em!

Hey you! Yes you! Put down the phone, iPod, iPad, game controller, hair dryer or whatever; plant your eye balls on me and stay there. You are not, I repeat, not the center of the family, the universe or anything else for that matter. Get over yourself. You're not as good as you think you are. You are, however, really irritating. Stop being a lazy, immature, self-centered, narcissistic, whining, ungrateful, pain in the butt cry baby and contribute to the family.

A little advice here; read Section 4 of this chapter, *Being a part or Being apart,* to find out what might just happen if you don't change your ways. You won't like what it says but no one cares. After all, no one likes the way you treat the family but you don't care, so it's even. Now give the book back to whoever gave it to and go do something that will benefit the whole family not just you for a change.

Ok, now that you've got the book back I want to say something about this creature living in your house. I told them they're not as good as they think they are. However, they may not be as bad as you and others think they are either. They just don't know how, or are unwilling to act their age or behave at the maturity level expected of them. They've probably caused a lot of bad feeling toward themselves from a lot of people. Some may hate them. They can lose what friends (real or fake) they have and cause the rest of the family to turn their backs on them due to their behavior. They're ignorant of the fact they make themselves look weak and stupid by acting the way they do. They're unaware of how many times they're made fun of and how much fun they're missing by being so hateful and arrogant.

Be firm with them and watch for cracks in their armor. They, like everyone else, want to be loved and appreciated. They're not appreciated now because of their actions. Being firm shows love. Not caving in shows you expect them to act as an equal member of the family. They want this but their maturity level is so low they resort to childish antics to get their way. If you see any weakening in their current behavior (like not pitching a stupid fit every time something doesn't go their way) it may mean their maturity level is rising. They may be getting tired of the way people feel about them. They may finally want to be considered a valuable, intelligent and cooperative member of the family – not the opposite. Look for it, then act on it. I wish you the best.

Chapter 7: Miscellaneous, Random, Generic, Non-Specific Stuff

Section 1: The Fault Game (Lay fault where it truly belongs and call it what it is!)

Blaming others for your mistakes means you're wrong again. In addition, you've probably ticked off the ones you've blamed which makes your situation worse. Bravo! No one buys the "it's not my fault" trick, at least not for long. We all make mistakes, but we'll lose control of whatever is left after our blunder if we try to pawn our part of the blame off on someone else. One fiasco should not lead to another. Remember, a blundering "duh" moment is a loss of some control. To get it back, you/we/I must admit your/our/my fault in it and rebuild what's been damaged.

Being exposed to a bad example then using it as an excuse for the exact same behavior is just plain stupid. Whatever you do is decided by you and done by you. You may have memories of bad behavior being performed around you but that's in the past. Concentrate on the here and now. Don't let the past control (there's that word again) who you are and what you do. Certainly, don't use the past actions of others as justification for your actions now. If you're so keenly aware of the past, use it to strengthen yourself. You know better than most the ugliness of that time. Don't continue the cycle.

I may sound hard core here and I don't mean to, but, come on, get help if you need it, it's out there. Seriously, I feel compassion for those who've suffered in their past. I want them to get the help they need and absolutely deserve. I'm not talking about them. I'm talking about people who purposely use their past as justification for their actions now when they are capable of resisting the urge to repeat the behavior.

Here's one some people use after they've done something stupidly dumb; "It's OK, I was drunk at the time." Bull Crap! It's never Ok, drunk or not. "Drunk" is not a justification. If being drunk is a justification and makes everything Ok, watch out. The next time you get punched out or your car keyed or someone puts their hands all over your significant other, just stand there with a goofy looking grin on your face and say, "Hey, it's cool, I see you're drunk; proceed." If you do interrupt their alcohol induced fun fest and they vomit liquids, solids and gasses all over you; wipe your face off and put that grin right back on. The best part is, there's no need to waste your time asking for an apology or payment to replace whatever they barfed on because they probably won't remember any of it. Come on, have a heart, it's OK, they were drunk, right?

A person who takes anything that is not theirs is called a thief and cannot be trusted. Thieves are too lazy to earn their own stuff. Do not let them in your house, car, yard etc. Don't put yourself and your stuff in a position to be ripped off. Once you've identified a person as a thief, a good deal of distance should be established between you, your valuables and them. I've only had a couple things stolen from me in my life and I can't say I liked it. I let my guard down a little and sure enough, "Presto," someone made something of mine disappear.

A thief is dishonest in thought and deed. Call me crazy (and some have) but if I can't trust someone not to take what is mine, depriving me of something I've earned, well, I simply don't have much to do with them anymore. I don't want to have to lock up everything I own that has any real or imaginary value just because so and so is coming over. I don't want to feel the need to check my glove box after I give so and so a ride to make sure my fancy tire pressure gauge or flashlight are still there. I don't need or want that kind of extra pressure.

A person who purposely says something they know is untrue is called a liar and cannot be trusted. Someone who will lie to you should just say "I hate you; you're not worth telling the truth to" and get it over with. There's no need to talk to them again or at a minimum, they (not you) must show proof that what they say is true from then on. Everything they say is now suspicious. Yes, I have a special place in my heart for liars. I've been lied to and I can't say I liked it. If I did, I'd be lying and that would be awkward right about now.

Truthfulness is essential to building relationships. What people see and hear from you should be exactly what they'll get all the time. No hidden agendas or tiny deceptions or secrets. Being honest isn't always easy. Sometimes what needs to be said would be more easily accepted if you bent the truth a little or broke it in half threw it away and made up something the person wants to hear. Problem is, the truth will not have changed and it will pop up at some later date.

If a person lies to me, I want to know why. I also want to know what the truth actually is since I didn't hear it from them. I try to allow myself to trust them but I can't muster up the same amount of trust as I had before. If their lying continues, I realize that's what I need to expect from them and no longer take their word for much of anything.

In a relationship, lying is a deal breaker for many people. Most give second chances. Some give third, fourth and fifth chances. A few give so many chances there's no use trying to count them. Each person has to decide for themselves how many times, if ever, they'll tolerate being lied to and just how important their feelings and emotions are. Here's a hint, they're very important. In fact, they're so important the other participant is the relationship should be protecting your feelings and emotions like Fort Knox protects gold. If they aren't, you have a problem. If they lie to you, it's the opposite of protection, its destruction.

How much destruction are you going to put up with before you act? How much destruction can you ignore and still try to trust? What will it take to set your "Too Much" alarm off? At what point will you be ready to free yourself from this kind of disrespect? If/when you're ready to act, realize you are not at fault, they are. If they tell you otherwise, you guessed it, they're lying.

Section 2: They're asking for it. (The Adult Translation)

When I was in the Air Force, I was a cop. As a cop, I wrote traffic tickets. When I say I wrote traffic tickets, I mean, I wrote a lot of traffic tickets. It didn't matter that stop signs are actually pretty large and red and reflective and stuck on a pole in plain sight with a word on it we all understand; some people just didn't see them. Well, actually, they did see them, they didn't see me seeing them roll or blow past them. Then, when I'd stop them, they'd let their attitudes loose as if I'd done something wrong. Some even asked the "quota" question. I always liked that one.

In the end, it came down to this; I (the cop) was sitting perfectly still and in plain sight (which was policy); the motor vehicle operator (not me and hopefully not a cop) did not stop at the aforementioned big red stop sign thingy. They got a ticket. I'd write it without concern for any real or imaginary quotas.

Before I'd trot back to my patrol car to write their ticket, some motorists would ask to be let go, freed if you will, from the upcoming negativities. They had seen the error of their ways and understood the necessity of stopping at the big red stop sign thingys from now on. They held no animosity toward me or police in general. In fact, they'd sometimes explain how they always wanted to be a cop or that their brother's best friend's uncle always wanted to be a cop. Yeah, yeah, yeah – just stay in your car and I'll be back with you in a couple minutes.

Some females (thinking they were in a movie or something) even asked if there was anything they could do (if you know what I mean) to get out of the ticket. My response would snap them back to reality when I'd explain what their question could be considered to insinuate, in a legal kind of way (if you know what I mean). Amazing, isn't it?

I had a female captain once who "cried" to try and get out of a ticket. She was driving three of her female captain friends around and happened to miss a big red stop sign thingy again (for the third time in a month I found out). Her "crying" was a less than stellar performance and very much unbecoming her rank. As she tried hard to squeeze out a tear and not mar her mascara, she asked me if it was really necessary to write her a ticket. She was, after all, an officer and was ferrying other officers to and fro which meant the car was full of, you guessed it, officers. I said it was. The "crying" stopped. Her half tear dried up and was replaced with threats. She wasn't going to let a measly Sergeant give her a ticket. She outranked me and that's all I or anyone else needed to know. She wasn't asking me, she was telling me, there would be no ticket writing going on. That was final, period.

When I finished writing the ticket and had given it to her she almost went back to crying, for real this time. Her commissioned officer passengers seemed rather embarrassed by her actions, as they should have been. I asked if she needed assistance moving back into traffic (another policy) she said she did not and she was on her way.

These examples simply point out the need to answer questions in the order they're received. The way I saw it then and see it now is this; I realize people have questions when they're pulled over for ignoring the big red stop sign thingy (or for any other reason). Cops need to answer the driver's first question, first.

The first question a cop is "asked" when a stop sign is not stopped at is this; "Excuse me police type person, would you please give me a ticket for this? If you don't, I'll keep doing it and next time I might hit an elementary school kid."

The speeders question is: "Pardon me sheriff's deputy so and so, may I have a citation. If I don't learn a lesson from this I might just kill someone or a lot of people or myself."

The maniac who passes someone at night, going uphill over a double yellow line is asking; "Would somebody, anybody, please stop me and ticket me, now? I am endangering my life and the lives of the people I pass and the people who may be just over the top of this hill. I need, want and deserve a ticket."

The answer to these types of first questions is simply, yes. That's final, period.

The lazy student is asking, "Oh wise and all-knowing teacher of mine, would you flunk me so I can take this class, which I hate, again next year?" What? That doesn't make sense to you and I but it does to a lazy student. They want to pass but don't want to put enough effort into it. Even though they're not doing much of anything, they are doing exactly what is necessary to do it all over again. They're asking to continue this academic agony for at least another nine months the following school year. They want to be in the class again with kids a year younger than they are, yeah, that's cool. Heck, they'll ask to flunk again and again just to prove their point. They hate the class, that's their point. Point taken, you flunk, have fun next year.

If you can believe it, the liar is asking; "Excuse me, would you please not trust what I say no matter how passionately I say it or how many times I say I really mean it and I wouldn't lie to you about this because it's too important? In fact, you shouldn't listen to me ever again since I'll probably just lie to you since I am a liar?"

To purposely say something you know is untrue and send people on their way trusting you is, in words; cowardly, hateful, disrespectful and of course, dishonest. It takes a long time to build trust. It sometimes only takes one lie to destroy it. Multiple lies spread the distrust to others, even if they've not been lied to themselves. Consistent lies ruin everything. If you never feel you can trust someone, your relationship is actually over. You can't ask them a question and trust their answer or believe anything they say anymore. Your relationship is corroded by dishonesty. Even if the liar apologizes, can you trust them? Only you know.

The liar doesn't care about your feelings or what might happen due to their purposeful dishonesty. They'll lie to get out of a lie and lie again until they can't keep track of them anymore. At that point, it'll all turn out to be your fault (which is a lie). The liar is asking not to be trusted and they shouldn't be.

Only after a time of rebuilding can trust begin again. If the liar truly wants to be believed they must apologize for their lies, in person and accept suspicion and checks of their honesty from then on. That's the only way to rebuild and restore a relationship torn apart by a liar. In my opinion, It would help if they'd just keep their mouths shut most of the time.

A boyfriend, girlfriend, fiancé or spouse who cheats on you is asking to be single again. When they cheat on you they've decided to give their attention to someone else. You aren't the sole "other" in the relationship, you've got company. These people no longer look at you as having enough love, encouragement and emotional support to fill their needs. They go out and find someone else, or many others, to fill their perceived voids. They may even say you drove them to cheat (which is a lie – they're a liar). Don't fall for it. They chose to cheat. They chose to cheat. Again, they chose to cheat.

What is cheating in a relationship? My views on this (and pretty much everything else) are cut and dry. To me, the cheaters actions translate to them saying; "I want to be single." I see cheating as participating in any activity with another person which excludes their boy/girlfriend, fiancé' or spouse. It does not have to be physical. Texting, e-mailing, eating meals, walking in the forest, on the beach or through a mine field, purposely staying late to "work," going on vacation together (yeah, people actually go on vacations; aka: "business trips" with their own personal home wrecker wannabe), calling each other at strange hours, calling each other at all and anything else which makes you feel cheated on. You and you alone decide (control) what cheating is, not them, or the other them.

You can forgive them and move ahead with your relationship if you wish. That's perfectly fine if it's what you want. They're at the mercy of your kind and generous heart at that point. Hopefully, you'll reach that decision after they've apologized, completely broken off the other relationship, removed all traces of the other person (phone numbers, e-mail address, *Facebook*, pictures, gift, etc.) from their/your life, apologized again, made it clear at their work they will not see or take messages from the other person and any other steps you deem necessary.

Hold on to something here; the two of you may consider moving. You can't make the relationship wrecker wannabe move. It's unfair for you to have to uproot but it might be for the best. It takes a special kind of person to do that. If your legitimate relationship is worth it to you, move.

A factoid to consider. Cheating is a relationship lie; therefore, the guilty party is a liar. Cheaters lie about cheating, which is a verbal lie. Therefore, the guilty party is a liar again but in a new way. They'll lie hundreds of times over months and years to continue their physical lie. They are professional liars and cheats and are asking, no begging, to be single again. Maybe they deserve the other person. They can build a new relationship on the foundation of lies the two of them have lived together. They shouldn't be surprised if/when their relationship crashes and burns. They deserve that too.

The kid not cleaning their room is asking their parents, "Would you be the most awesome parents in the whole wide world and take my internet privileges away for the next 600 years?" They ask this in subtle ways like; covering their bedroom floor with their wardrobe in a wrinkled mosaic pattern, growing penicillin from ancient scraps of peanut butter sandwiches left under their bed, producing odors which are clearly visible to the naked eye and creating modern art masterpieces from their bed sheets, a chair and miscellaneous object you've never seen before. By the way; the Internet and all other things your kids have, beyond their basic needs, are privileges, not rights.

Translate people's actions into a question. You may find, they've been "asking for it" for a long time.

Section 3: Your Thank Account (How much do you owe?)

The title of this one gives it away so well I don't have to write anything, but I will.

We try to teach our kids to say thank you as soon as they can utter the words. We ask them "what do we say" and they respond with something like "tank euw, gamma"; very cute.

It's not very long before we're reminding them to say thank you. After that, many give up hope of ever hearing it again. We tell ourselves they're thankful, they just don't say it. Well, they need to and so do we.

None of us say thank you enough. Not just as a reaction to something nice that's happened but the explanatory thank you that expresses what we're thankful for and to whom. Yes, we feel thankful; we just don't say anything about it. We owe others our thanks.

You know darn well there's at least one person out there you should say thank you to right now, probably more. If your thank account is full, or half full, or has a little bit in it, give what's inside it away. It's not like a bank account where you try to spend a little and save a lot, it's the opposite. Thank accounts should be empty at all times.

As soon as someone does something worth being thanked for it's a deposit into your account. All you have to do is withdrawal the same amount and give it back; a good thing is done for you – a thank you is given back. Simple. The less you give back, the more full your thank account gets. Eventually, people might stop making deposits (doing nice things for you) because they never receive anything in return. If there's no room left in your account for new deposits it's your fault.

Kids owe their parents the most thanks I think. After all, without their parents, they'd be naked, starving and without the newest and bestest "iThing" on the market to impress their fellow naked and ill-fed peers. Kids don't comprehend how much effort (emotional, financial, physical and spiritual) it requires to raise them. They don't understand how much parents worry about them. They don't know the power of the thank you.

During the years Cathy and I coached the color guard we did many different things with the kids to clarify the importance of being thankful.

To be accepted as a guardsman, many kids had to pass color guard boot camp (our version of try outs). During boot camp "recruits" endured a variety of behavior modifications, most of which are designed to kick start their "thank you" motors. For example, the following behaviors were no, no's; speaking at a normal volume, moving at a normal velocity, leaning against stuff, having their hands in their pockets, looking around, having personal space, doing things their own way, mumbling, referring to adults as "hey you," saying "uhm," eating food they like or can identify, avoiding the irritations of gravity, mud and water and a host of other forbidden actions.

The aforementioned modifications were enforced by the careful employment of the following techniques. These techniques were designed to motivate the recruits to be thankful for what they already had. They were administered to the energy drink propelled youth to unceremoniously strip them of their individual wants and desires. Recruits were then issued my opinion of how they should, could and definitely would behave.

This was the Senior Drill Instructor briefing before one of our boot camps officially began. Prior to this there had already been about 45 minutes of running off then back on the bus the recruits arrived in, sprinting in and back out of the building numerous times and "games" played with the bags of personal belongings they had brought; all to set the proper mood.

Questions, anyone? I didn't think so. Establishment of the proper mood; Check!

It takes a well-trained eye to see that I'm actually quite pleased with the recruit's progress at this point during boot camp. Of course, I didn't tell them that until it was all over. When boot camp is over the recruits are lavished with praise and motivation for their accomplishments. They have survived the games, passed the tests and will wear the Color Guard shoulder tab on their uniforms identifying them as Color Guardsmen. The Senior Drill Instructor is no longer the horrible beast they once thought he was; he is now their trainer, mentor and protector.

No one ever asks; "What?" after a Drill Instructor speaks. This little rant was the direct result of a recruit not ending his answer with the title, "Ma'am" after speaking to a female. In boot camp, that's a definite no, no.

The techniques used were the following; recruits yelled almost everything they said at the top of their lungs, they moved as fast as humanly possible at a dead sprint, they stood at attention unless otherwise directed, they stood and sat pressed against each other on all sides, they used proper titles such as "Sir," "Ma'am," "Mr.," "Mrs.," "Miss," "Gentleman," "Lady" and so on, they used only actual words; no grunts, whines, wheezes, shoulder shrugs, etc. and said "please" and "thank you" every time it was appropriate.

For lunch they were in the sun eating ¼ of an unheated military field ration while lying on their stomachs propped up on their elbows. They did this while in a tight circle with their shoulders touching and drank plastic tasting water from canteens. Instructors, guests and parents ate hot, delivered pizza and drank soft drinks or cold water while sitting on lawn chairs in the shade.

Recruits accepted yelling by instructors (who were inches from their faces) for the slightest infraction. This was done at a decimal level near the sound barrier breaking point. Recruits also forced their bodies up and down a hill in varying ways while five-gallon buckets of water hit them like waves. This turned the hill into mud soup and the recruits into mud soup covered appreciative young people. Actually, the kids loved the hill most of all out of boot camp. Go figure.

These requirements had an effect on the kids. They became thankful for how their lives had been before showing up a 9:00 AM that morning and for what they would return to after 5:00 PM in the afternoon the same day. Yep, it only took eight hours to convince them they'd had it pretty good and had not shown the proper amount of thanks to those who were providing them such a cushy life style.

What caused the change? For some it was the "shock and awe" of the first hour of boot camp, for others it happened through a lecture or a story. Many had a revelation that their unappreciative behavior and lack of thankfulness was not only noticed and disliked by their parents but it was holding their parents back from giving them more responsibilities and freedoms.

All recruits received the hill's message loud and clear. The final challenge required them to crawl up the hill using only their arms. They had to drag their legs along for the ride. This was done after they'd spent a considerable amount of time and almost all their energy repeatedly walking, crawling and rolling down, then back up the hill. Remember, the hill was muddy and slick. It's was hard.

Once they'd all slithered their way to the top I'd tell them how appreciative they should have been about their lives, their parents and the things they'd been taking for granted. I'd inform them they shouldn't have been complaining about so many things. After all, it could always get worse. Then I'd tell them they had to crawl up the hill again the same way, but had to do so faster than the first time or they'd keep doing it until they were faster.

You'd be amazed how fast they throw themselves up that hill. They'd get to the top and actually go back down again to help others who were struggling. They had to crawl back up with them but they didn't care. They weren't going to let their fellow mud buddies fail. There were shouts of motivation from instructors, the kids and their parents. There was clapping, cheering and happy crying as mud flew all over the place.

The kids felt a sense of power and accomplishment they'd never felt before. They had conquered the hill and their own

Ladies and gentlemen, welcome to "The Hill."

wimpy attitudes. They appreciated what had happened to them as individuals and as a group. They realized their lives weren't bad at all, in fact, they were pretty good. The best part was, they saw their parents in a different way; the proper way.

The kids were tougher and thankful of the instructors for pushing them and their parents for providing for them. From that point on, when they faced a challenge at school or in their personal lives they'd be able to say, "I can handle this – it could be worse – I could be crawling up the hill."

Section 4: $1,000 (Is it really necessary?)

One thousand dollars is always necessary, especially if you want to buy $1,000 worth of stuff. I want to use $1K (as I'll call it) for a different purpose. It's now a motivator. A motivator for whatever it is you should be doing but for some reason are not.

I've used this with teens with good results. I just say I'll give them $1,000 if they turn in the paperwork I've asked for, be on time for, well, everything, do their chores at home without whining or crying, eat their vegetables, brush their teeth, yadda, yadda, yadda and so on. I tell them, heck yeah, you'd do all those things for $1K, but exactly why should it take $1K to get you to do what you should be doing anyway? Other people do these things and much more simply because they need to be done, sans cash award.

It's a question of maturity and priorities. Some people aren't mature enough to do what's needed for the simple reason it needs to be done. They must have some other incentive. I didn't say they needed another incentive, they just want one. Others have their priorities messed up. Check out "Needs and Wants" for extra goodies on that one.

We all need to find ways to motivate ourselves past substandard behavior. We should find out within ourselves what an action is "worth" thus giving it value. We already either get paid from our jobs or are being provided for by our parents. We can't expect to be given a tip every time we do the normal, mundane things of life. If that happened, we'd all be overachievers raking in the bucks at $1K a pop. Let's get real. We're all slackers sometimes (yes, even me). Slacking off shouldn't be the norm though.

If I gave you $1K to be more appreciative and loving toward your spouse would you do it? How about $1K for managing your money better (a little ironic isn't it), there could be a $1K reward for taking better care of yourself (the old diet and exercise thing again), $1K could come your way for helping with the housework, you could be "in the money" if you'd only, you can fill in the rest.

The problem is, no one is going to pay you for this stuff. Your payment, if you must have one, is the satisfaction you're doing your part and aren't a burden to others. That should be enough. Actually, it is.

Section 5: 80 Per centers (Hey, pick up my slack!)

Come on, you know the kind of people I'm talking about; the ones who always leave just a little of their work undone so someone else does it for them. It's usually not enough to make a big difference but it still needs to be done, so you, "the good work ethic people" end up doing it.

Listen up. The 80 per centers have control of a little bit of you by simply walking away from the last 20 per cent of their work. Here's a thought. Stop it; doing their work I mean. It's irritating to see things undone but it isn't yours to do. Let it go, to coin a movie song title I've heard way too much. I wouldn't even tell them you've decided to take back control of your work time and effort. If your boss(es) are worth their titles, they'll figure it out and hopefully make a boss-like decision against the 80 per center.

But what if the 80 per center asks you to do their last 20 per cent for them? Answer: Big Fat No. Of course, make it come out softer than that since 80 per centers can be a sensitive lot. You could say, "I've got enough to do and couldn't possibly do your work for you, you lazy troll." Hmm, still needs work I think. Anyway, you'll figure it out.

Here's another one. Have you ever been told, "I'll call you back" and the call never happens? Yeah, that one makes you want to choke the stuffing out of a fluffy teddy bear. That call makes up the last 20 per cent of their work. So, what do you and I do? We call them back. Where's a fluffy teddy bear when you need one?

Section 6: Bosses (Are they good enough for you?)

Here's a twist. I realize my boss now and all my previous bosses have expected pretty much the same things from me; be on time, don't miss too many days, do my job – my whole job – and nothing but my job. I do the best I can at work and always have. I can't say the same for some of the bosses I've had throughout my many years of toil.

The main reason for this was, you guessed it dear reader, control; actually, the lack of it. My worst bosses all had one thing in common; they lacked the ability or just didn't try hard enough to control the "who" and "what" which was under their control. Ironic huh? The "who" I'm talking about were some of my co-workers. The ones I call 80 percent-ors. Remember them? The "what" are explained in detail below.

Being on time. We've all had the misfortune of having co-workers who don't co-work with us. When they finally get to work, they mosey in with the same excuses or no excuse at all and begin their shift. This takes place after we've had to do our and their jobs until they make their illustrious arrival. Coming back late from breaks is another neat trick these people pull. Don't forget leaving early, wondering off or taking forty-five minutes for a restroom break. Hey, if you need that much time, go to the ER or lay off the burritos for a while.

Not missing too many days. At least they got to work, right? That in itself is an accomplishment. Fridays get missed a lot so the week-end can start earlier. Mondays are missed a lot because the week-end hasn't stopped yet; at least the headache and nausea hasn't. Just how many absences, past the maximum number of absences allowed, is allowable anyway? I always thought it was zero. As it turns out, I always thought wrong.

Doing the job – the whole job. Once they're firmly planted at their designated area, as far as working goes, some do and some don't. Most of the time I've seen these types do a "fifty percent - glutinous maximus" job at best. Even if they've been employed longer than others, they'll ask how to do things or simply do them in the shortest way possible no matter how incomplete or wrong it may be. When talking about the worst offenders; to me, them not being at work is about the same as them being at work.

Nothing but the job. Let's see, instead of working there's talking to this person or that person or any other person not related to their job, various manipulations of their cell phones ability to distract them from their job, leaving for parts unknown away from their job, interfering with another person's job, daydreaming about their next job and many more non-job-related activities.

You might be a little confused here. This topic is supposed to be about bosses after all. Well, it is, believe me. You see, the blame for this kind of behavior from an employee can and should be placed on them, but not only them. It also can and should be placed on their boss.

This behavior has many negative affects at the work place; frustration, resentment and hatred from other employees, a downward spiral in productivity, a flushing of morale, company pride – forget about it, the obvious glare of favoritism, the (right or wrong) assumption of non-work-related relationships between the habitually absent, late, unproductive and under skilled employee and the boss who allows it and so on.

Bosses, whether they're called supervisors, managers, foremen or forewomen, coaches, team leaders, or whatever new name is being used now days for the same level of responsibility, have an obligation. Their obligation is to all their employees, as well as, the company which has promoted them. They're supposed to train, evaluate, correct and fire/terminate/sack and in all other ways remove the habitually absent, late, unproductive and under skilled employee from the aforementioned company. This also removes them from the habitually present, on time, productive and skilled employees who actually want their jobs.

Bosses are supposed to have control over their employees and their departments. The most basic element of control is the behavior of the employees as it related to their work. Without controlling the behavior of employees, the employees will do as little as possible. It's kinda human nature. I think it's called the path of least resistance.

Being the boss means correcting problem employees, documenting their actions, retraining them if necessary and removing them as soon as it becomes clear they cannot or will not conduct themselves properly. The short version is; keep the best people, boot out the rest and replace them with new ones who want to be the best. It does not mean acting like nothing is going on hoping they'll improve on their own. Bosses should be fired for that nonsense.

What causes a boss to do basically nothing to control the obvious problem child in their midst? Some reasons I've witnessed are; they're just lazily "earning" their pay checks, they're basically clueless as to what a boss is, they're the owner's son or daughter, they're intimidated by being the boss and by their employees, they're a drama king or queen, they and the problem employee are BFFs, they're having an affair with the problem employee or they messed up their last department and were transferred before they caused any more damage.

Back to the twist. We're used to feeling the stress of trying to be good enough for our bosses and the company we work for. That's normal and appropriate but I think there's more. In my humble opinion, our bosses should feel the same stress about being good enough for us. I have high standards for myself. I also have high standards for my bosses. If they don't measure up, I start looking elsewhere for a job.

If my boss won't fix the problems they're responsible for and their bosses won't fix them, then the problems will never be fixed. If the problems are bad enough, no amount of money or preferred shifts or coupons or t-shirts or not so catchy slogans will compensate for the misery they cause.

If you leave a job because of an inferior boss, don't think of it as your failure. You're boss has failed you and you've taken back control. Yes, you'll have to start over somewhere but it might be just the job you've been looking for and deserve to have. You deserve to be productive, appreciated and happy enough in your work. Your boss should do what is necessary to make that happen for all their employees – at least the ones who show up, on time and do their job, their whole job and nothing but their job.

Section 7: Color (It's only skin deep)

The "King of Pop" wrote something in one of his many hit songs that's simple, direct and motivational. He wrote that he wasn't going to live his life being a color. Good stuff right there. Some people still believe, as ridiculous as it is, that the color of another person's skin means that person is from a different race or is automatically inferior. This is determined because their shade of skin is not the same as the observers' shade of skin. What kind of doofusology is this?

Humans are humans no matter what shade. Some humans are good and some are bad, no matter what shade. Some make great contributions to others and some hurt others, no matter what shade. Some will be remembered long after they're gone and others will be given the last name "Doe" when they leave this earth, no matter what shade.

I've written about my sister-in-law Alma a little already but here's more. She is extremely intelligent and has a work ethic (like my wife's) that makes her an outstanding employee. She was a star athlete in high school and at The U.S. Military Academy at West Point. She's an awesome wife and mother. She's funny, caring and beautiful. We all love her like crazy.

But, how could this be? She has a different shade. I'll tell you how this can be. Alma's character is what we love. You have to look inside a person to see their character, not just stare at the surface. Some would say she's black or African American or Negro or whatever shade description they choose to use. Her shade, if you must have one, is Hulse. That's all we need. Every person should be judged on the content of their character. Wait. I've heard that somewhere before. Someone smart must have said it – no matter what shade.

Section 8: Heroes (They're not who you think.)

The term hero is thrown around a lot, too much in fact. People are called heroes for all kinds of reasons but few are heroic reasons. People do great things, even extraordinary and exceptional things, but that's not heroism. Great accomplishments are just that and the people achieving them should be recognized. It doesn't mean they're a hero.

I don't look at actors, athletes or other celebrities as heroes. I like what they do and hope they continue but they're not my heroes. Who can argue that Al Pacino isn't a great actor? Michael Jordan was great in every aspect of professional basketball (and in pitching socks and underwear). Mohamed Ali was "The Greatest" and Peyton Manning was great at throwing a football exactly where he wanted it to go, but none are heroes. Elvis Presley, Steve Perry and Whitney Huston, 'nuff said, but even they don't measure up to hero in my book (and this is my book).

My heroes have things in common. For example, they give of themselves to help others. I'm not talking about talent or a million dollars given away here and there out of a bank account with a few hundred million in it. I mean, really give of what they have in a sacrificial way or a way in which they take it upon themselves to protect others. My heroes are those who help reestablish control where it has been lost.

Police Officers control evidence at crime scenes so a proper investigation can be made to arrest the guilty. They control the aggression and violence of others directed toward the innocent. They run toward gun fire when everyone else, and all good reason says, to run the other way. They will lay down their lives for me. The police are my heroes.

Firemen control the spread of fires and extinguish them. They run into burning buildings to save others. They pull people from burning cars about to explode. They battle wild fires and can deliver your baby; burning buildings, exploding cars, wild fires and babies. Firemen are my heroes.

Paramedics, EMTs, First Responders and anyone else in that category with a title I'm not familiar with, save people's lives, plain and simple. These angels on earth are my heroes.

Teachers control their classrooms to promote the best learning environment possible. They do this while some students go out of their way to disrupt, be disrespectful, or at a minimum, do nothing in class. They make their own syllabuses, lesson plans, activities and tests. They grade work turned in and chase down work forgotten, lost, thrown away, burned or flushed.

They answer the same questions over and over again. They acknowledge good work, help those who haven't quite got it yet and are amazed at the insights some students have who not only get it, but get it with clarity.

They encourage every student, even those whose response to everything is, "whatever." They use discipline when needed and listen to students who have no one to talk to. They're praised and yelled at by parents and have state standards breathing down their necks. In some cases, they're "graded" as teachers on the performance of their students. Some student's efforts are, well, whatever. Not a way to measure the teacher I don't think. Teachers are my heroes.

I feel the same about Pastors, Doctors and people who help others with special needs. Those with special needs are heroes as well. They overcome so much to accomplish what we take for granted.

I was a "hugger" for a track and field meet involving special needs kids while I was in the Air Force. All I did was wait for whoever was in my lane to cross the finish line. I didn't say they had to be first or second, they just had to cross, if they could. Some stopped part way down the track. That was their finish line. No matter where they placed in the race or what place on the track they stopped, they got a hug. Not an ordinary hug. I'm talking a serious mega-hug. We hugged, jumped up and down, high fived, did a little dance and hugged again. They smiled so big and laughed so loud it brought tears to my eyes. They had accomplished something big and I was blessed to be a part of it. Special needs folks are my heroes.

I even have non-human heroes. Military Working Dogs known as MWDs and civilian police dogs, sometimes called K9s, are my four-legged heroes. They do what they're told, immediately, to the best of their ability and without thought of their own safety. They will only stop performing their duty when they "retire" or if they are killed in the line of duty. Their loyalty is without question. K9s are my heroes.

My Super Heroes are (you've probably figured this out already) our men and women serving in the Armed Forces. They volunteer to serve and don't get paid much unless their sleeves are full of stripes or their shoulders carry around oak leaf clusters, eagles or stars.

Basic Training/Boot Camp is unpleasant to say the least. Technical training is stressful and exciting and allows the young service member to perform tasks usually not allowed in the civilian world for a person their age.

The responsibility level and level of accountability for a 19-year service member often exceeds that of civilian supervisors and managers who are 20 years older. I was 19 when I joined. By the time I hit 20 years of age I was performing law enforcement duties, had graduated from ground combat training (infantry school), passed my secondary level of on-the-job training and had survived my first of many unit level combat skill evaluations (two weeks of war games). See what I mean? The amount of knowledge, accuracy, organization, problem solving, respect and adherence to regulations and procedures is truly incredible; even for those who have half of their first enlistment to go.

Many of the jobs in the military are, of course, combat related. Take all the aforementioned requirements and add a pistol, rifle or machine gun, grenades, rocket launcher, parachute, scuba gear, satellite communications equipment, medic bag, maybe the need to speak another language or the knowledge of another country's customs; now mix it all up and slap on a helmet. Now order them to leave home for years and drop them smack dab in the middle of harm's way. That's a service member. That's my hero.

You don't have to agree with where our service members are deployed, why they're deployed or your tax money being spent to deploy them. Remember, they're following orders and would no doubt rather be home with their families and friends. They're sacrificing for us so we don't have to.

While I'm on the subject, if you don't agree with our foreign policies, tell an elected official about it. If you don't like their response (or lack of one) fire them. The vote is a powerful thing. Don't treat a service member like it was their idea to go here or there. It wasn't. Just thank them for their service, wish them strength and safety, maybe shake their hand and press on with your day happy in the knowledge you just met a true American Hero.

Section 9: Wants and Needs (Not in that order.)

Take a piece of paper and draw a line down the middle. Write "NEEDS" and "WANTS" at the top of the respective halves. Now write down what you feel your needs and wants truly are.

Your needs will be very few and pretty much the same as everyone else. Your wants will be many and specific to your personality. Your needs are immediate and will never change. Your wants can change with trends. Your needs will keep you alive and safe; your wants will keep you entertained and popular.

People with "Prioritive Dyslexia" put wants before needs. They may fall behind on their payments then ask you to help them pay their bills or buy groceries or gas. This will be done while they sport a new haircut and color and after you've read about them bragging on *Facebook* about their new 300-inch TV and video game purchases. Yes, the fact they are on face book means they have a computer and internet and now you know a video game system, all of which are wants not needs. They want you to sacrifice your money so they don't sacrifice theirs.

You never have to pay for another person's needs when they have money to do so but choose to pay for their wants instead.

You also never have to pay for their wants, why on earth would you? Oh yeah, if you give in they probably won't pay you back, that would be a need.

When starting a relationship, it might be wise (and a little weird I admit) to have your prospective other do this, then compare your lists. If their need list requires two pages and yours has half a dozen items on it you are in for some problems. Similar lists suggest similar priorities. The more different the lists the more one of you may have to sacrifice to keep the peace. It's Ok if the lists are different but the relationship will be lived through those differences and that can be tough.

Section 10: Money (Where does it all go?)

See *Wants*.

Section 11: Discrimination (Don't do it but profile like crazy!)

A rather important disclaimer is on its way. When I say "profile" I am not saying racially profile or politically profile or socially profile or religiously profile. That wouldn't be profiling, that would be discrimination and I just said don't do that inside those parentheses up there. Ok, good talk – carry on.

Discrimination is the true sign of fear. Fear of the unknown, of differences, of the possibility of not being as good as someone else, say, in business, athletics or academics. It's usually caused by the outward appearance of the body's largest organ, the skin. Yeah, that's a good way to determine if a person is this or that. Don't discriminate, it makes you look stupid, and weak, and uneducated, and out of touch, and backward, and so on.

Profiling people is not discrimination, its evaluation. One dictionary defines it as; "the use of personal characteristics or behavior patterns to make a generalization about a person." That sounds good to me.

When do we profile other humanoids? Answer: Whenever they're around. Why do we profile humanoids? Answer: Because they're around. How do we profile humanoids? Answer: By observation with our eyes and the use of other senses, such as, hearing and unfortunately, smell. Realistically, your "gut" will tell you who to profile.

Let's look at profiling as it pertains to personal safety. A guy wearing a professional sports team sweatshirt and jeans, walking past you to the store looks harmless and probably is. On the other hand, the guy at 9:00am wearing a shredded shirt and filthy jeans, covered in tattoos and piercings, having just bounced his (still lit) cigarette off his baby's stroller, who stinks of beer from 20 feet away and is screaming profanities at his (there's a name here I won't use) may be perfectly harmless, but he does not profile that way.

Don't get me wrong, wearing torn clothes, having tattoos and piercings and smoking are not crimes. Being intoxicated in public and endangering a baby is. Screaming profanities is disturbing the peace. He profiles as an unclean, disrespectful, narcissistic, oblivious, alcoholic, overbearing, aggressive and abusive jerk. It's time to have your radar on and all systems ready for, whatever. Whatever, almost never comes, but his profile warrants a defensive mindset.

Ok, my example for the jerk was a little over the top. How about three teen age boys walking between cars in a parking lot looking inside the windows? All the while they're talking so loud you can't help but notice them (that's what they're going for). They're spouting off profanity and making vulgar comments about the women (and little girls) they see. They'll ask, "what are you lookin' at" to anyone caught spying in their direction and head straight for them a few steps then head somewhere else. Hmm, let me think; nope, I don't like it.

I'd profile them as three people who are not going to get close to my wife, kids or grandkids. I will watch them as we walk to the store keeping myself between my family and the three walking and talking hemorrhoids. I'm not intimidated, afraid or nervous. I'm too busy being the sheep dog (see, Sheep, Sheep Dogs and Wolves).

My wife and I have a system in place if a situation goes south. If I feel there is real danger closing in and don't think she can get away safely, I'll say "Emergency Stay." She immediately tucks herself behind me, holding on to my belt and moves in step with me to prevent tripping. Her entire body is behind mine. I am the shield. We move away from the threat.

As soon as I think she can get away safely, or if I think so at the beginning, I'll say, "Emergency Go." In that instant, my wife will leave in a direction behind me, staying low and moving very fast but carefully, weaving left to right so as not to move in a straight line. Whenever possible, she will maneuver around an object to make it a barrier between herself and the threat.

The point is, she goes from being either beside me or tucked in behind me, to gone – fast! I stay behind, moving backwards in the direction she has gone, with my eyes on the threat. I continue until I find her. Non-action is not an option, neither is hesitation.

If your gut tells you to pay attention to someone or a group, do it. Don't live your life in a state of paranoia, freaking out at every little noise or from the sight of someone who looks different. Just keep your head out of the clouds and scan for wolves. If an emergency arises, take out your shield and stand your ground.

Men, specifically fathers, should profile the young scholars who wish to date their daughters. You may think there isn't a single boy on earth who is worthy of daddy's little girl, and of course, you'd be right. However, she will expect to date at some point so you might as well be ready.

Here's the short version: Your daughter must know (no later than two or three days after birth) what your profile is and is not for a dateable boy. She should grow up with this understanding clearly embedded in her mind (you may want to paint it on her bedroom walls just to be safe). When she is old enough to date, she will bring a boy home who exactly meets your profile in every possible way. He will politely and respectfully ask permission to date your daughter. You will deny him. It's just that easy, hee, hee.

Just profile people when your gut tells you to do so, don't assume anything and be a shield carrying sheep dog.

Section 12: Taking Time Off (AKA: Quitting)

The body relaxes from lack of activity. The mind tries to predict how long the time off will be but really doesn't know. Other activities may replace the old one thus filling up the time needed to resume. After a short time, the body wants to stay relaxed and the mind agrees. After a while the body no longer desires to do what it once did and the mind says you are too far behind to start again. After enough time has passed (different for each person) the body is completely satisfied being relaxed (or involved in something new) and the mind is convinced that the time off was the right thing to do and you probably shouldn't have been doing the other thing in the first place.

The mind of course, is wrong. You are not that far behind and it was worth doing. When you really think about it, you'll feel regret for not sticking with it. You'll estimate where you'd be if you had kept going. You'll wonder why you ever stopped.

Years later the stories will begin about what you were going to do if you had stayed with it. You might even show pictures of yourself back then. Sad. You'll have to answer the question, "Why'd you quit?" First, you'll correct them by explaining you didn't quit but simply took time off and you didn't return because, well, you'll make up something.

Section 13: Good Things (Looking Forward)

Real quick; try to always have something good to look forward to. Listen up now, this is important; put it on your calendar and don't let anything mess with it. It doesn't have to be a massively expensive week-long vacation extravaganza; it could be renting a movie or two, ordering a pizza or two and making a homemade hot fudge sundae - or two. How about a manicure and/or pedicure ladies? Shopping anyone? Dudes; fishing, computer gaming with 1,000 of your closest gaming buddies or just choking down chili and cheese covered brats and a family sized bag of chips while sitting on the front porch in your bath robe? Whatever floats your boat, do it to the max! Good times.

Even a small distraction from the daily grind is a welcome one. Remember to put it on your calendar and keep the appointment. Do this at least once a month. It's your relaxation, rejuvenation and "all about me" time and you truly deserve it.

Time to go (Wrapping it up.)

Wow, you made it. I hope you enjoyed my book and maybe got a tip or two about taking back the control you've lost. I hope you're energized, motivated and determined to do what must be done.

Remember, you're an extremely important person and deserve to be happy in all areas of your life. Control of those areas can be the difference between feeling miserable and feeling the happiest you've ever been. Control – It should be yours - Take it back!

I wish you the very best now and for the future.

Sincerely,

Seth

Connect with Seth

www.controlmeasureslifecoaching.com

controlmeasureslc@gmail.com

Other books from Gold Rush Publishing

www.GoldRushPub.com

Semicolon; Memoir of a Colon Cancer Survivor

By Mark T. Arsenault
Semicolon takes a frank but humorous, and often witty, look at the procedures and events surrounding one man's journey through colorectal cancer. Mark takes on the serious, at times frightening, and potentially deadly issues. It will enlighten and entertain you at the same time. *$14.99; ISBN-13: 978-1890305055*

The Truth About Self-Publishing Your Book

By Mark T. Arsenault
Learn the truth about self-publishing from a best-selling and award winning self-published author, Mark T. Arsenault. The book takes you step by step through the process of self-publishing your book, from choosing a topic to write about to marketing your new book to boost sales. *$9.99; ISBN-13: 978-1890305123*

Think Up!

By Mark T. Arsenault
Best-selling author Mark T. Arsenault, presents *Think Up!*, a collection of short articles and blog posts designed to help readers look beyond their circumstances, achieve a positive mindset and reach their goals. *$9.99; ISBN-13: 978-1890305161*

Mad Learning: 6th Grade Spelling Words Puzzle Book

By Mark T. Arsenault
Contains 90 entertaining and engaging word search puzzles. Puzzles containing all 6th Grade Wonder Words, plus challenge words! 20x20 word find grids, each containing about 25 words. Solutions for each puzzle are included in the back. *$9.99; ISBN-13: 978-1890305185*

The Jen-Jen Chronicles

The Jen-Jen Chronicles is a juvenile fiction series by best-selling author Mark T. Arsenault, that follows Jennifer, a young, pre-teen girl who lives with her best friend and her family. While written for younger readers, the books deal with the subjects of neglect, substance abuse, and other serious topics, in an age-appropriate way. A great way to discuss issues with children in a guardianship, foster family, or adopted family situation.

A New Home (The Jen-Jen Chronicles, Book One)

By Mark T. Arsenault

Jennifer's daddy sends her to her friend Danielle's for the weekend while he looks for a new place to live. That begins Jennifer's new journey of discovery, in which she learns the true meaning of home and family. *$7.99; ISBN-13: 978-1890305291*

Back on Track (The Jen-Jen Chronicles, Book Two)

By Mark T. Arsenault

Jennifer lives with her best friend. Her dad promised her a birthday party at the jump park but he hasn't visited her in weeks. She's excited for the party but mad at her dad for not visiting her. Can she can trust the Arnolds enough to share her true feelings with them? *$7.99; ISBN-13: 978-1890305390*

Blue October (The Jen-Jen Chronicles, Book Three)

By Mark T. Arsenault

School is out in October. Halloween is coming up and so is the end date of Jennifer's dad's consent to stay at the Arnolds'. Jennifer has a medical condition that's getting worse. Will Jennifer get treated? Will she finally go back to live with her dad? *$7.99; ISBN-13: 978-1890305406*

Parental advisory: While written for younger readers, The Jen-Jen Chronicles deals with the subjects of neglect, substance abuse, and other serious topics. This book may not be suitable for some children without parental guidance. We encourage parents/guardians to discuss the story and topics in this book with your child.

www.ingramcontent.com/pod-product-compliance
Lightning Source LLC
LaVergne TN
LVHW051827080426
835512LV00018B/2761